T0311237

HIGH
RETURNS

~⁀ *from* ⁀~

LOW RISK

a remarkable stock market paradox

HIGH
RETURNS

❦ *from* ❧

LOW RISK

a remarkable stock market paradox

PIM VAN VLIET
JAN DE KONING

WILEY

This edition first published 2017
© 2017 Pim van Vliet and Jan de Koning

Registered office
John Wiley & Sons Ltd, The Atrium, Southern Gate, Chichester, West Sussex, PO19 8SQ, United Kingdom

For details of our global editorial offices, for customer services and for information about how to apply for permission to reuse the copyright material in this book please visit our website at www.wiley.com.

Library of Congress Cataloging-in-Publication Data is available

A catalogue record for this book is available from the British Library.

ISBN 978-1-119-35105-4 (hbk) ISBN 978-1-119-35108-5 (ebk)
ISBN 978-1-119-35109-2 (ebk) ISBN 978-1-119-35718-6 (ebk)

Cover Design: Wiley
Cover Image: © Antar Dayal/Getty Images

Set in 12/15.5 Adobe Jenson Pro by Aptara Inc., New Delhi, India
Printed and bound by CPI Group (UK) Ltd, Croydon, CR0 4YY

C9781119351054_120324

Contents

Introduction

THIS BOOK REVEALS A STORY ABOUT THE STOCK MARKET WHICH WILL CHANGE THE WAY YOU THINK ABOUT INVESTING. It is a story about a paradox I stumbled upon many years ago, one that still amazes me today. It is the story of an 'inconvenient truth' for economics professors as it turns their models upside down. A delusional story for professional investors who are managing other people's money. It's also a personal story which will make you smile and wonder. But most importantly, it's a story that will help you become a better investor, as it describes how to turn scientific insights into profits. It is the modern stock market equivalent of 'the tortoise and the hare': a remarkable tale of how low-risk stocks beat high-risk stocks.

My goal is to explain this stock market paradox to you as I would explain it to my father. He is a retired businessman with stock market investing experience. Although he is not an expert in finance, he is a wise man with an entrepreneurial mindset. He has taught our family to respect classical virtues such as prudence, patience, and persistence. Over the years I have discovered that there is a close link between these principles and successful investing. By referring to his values, I will explain this paradox in an understandable way. If my father can understand this story, you might understand it as well.

My wife is a surgeon, and her field of medicine has been transformed by the 'evidence-based' approach. Every pill she prescribes is extensively tested and empirically validated. You will agree that this makes sense, since it directly affects our physical health. However, when it comes to our financial health we are not yet that advanced. When somebody makes a profitable investment, it's not so easy to explain whether it's down to good luck or pure skill. Investors often quickly draw conclusions based on too little statistical evidence. Luckily, things are starting to change for the better. Evidence-based investing – applying thoroughly tested investment theories to portfolio construction – is on the rise. In this book I will apply this scientific approach to stock market investing and show you significant results that justify its effectiveness going back as far as 1929.

But this book is not all about science and applied wisdom. In fact, it starts with an impatient and overconfident teenager who tries his luck on the stock market. It's the story of a young academic who stumbles upon a huge but puzzling investment paradox. Later, as an ambitious investment manager, he translates this academic theory into a multi-billion-dollar investment strategy. At each stage, he understands more and more about why low-risk stocks are shunned by most investors and how this behavior explains the existence of this paradox.

In today's world you can rely less and less on government help in meeting your pension requirements, so the answer is to start investing yourself. For this reason, my father manages his own pension portfolio and I invest for my kids' future. I hope this remarkable story about risk can help you take responsibility for your own financial well-being and that of others.

This is also why I believe that, after writing numerous academic research papers on this subject, it is time to tell the story to a broader audience of investors. People like my father and you. So I have written a book about this great stock market paradox that

I hope is simple and easy to understand. Drawing on my experience as a researcher and fund manager, I will translate complex academic theory into a simple investment strategy, which you can directly implement to shape your financial future. This narrative is a story that I have told many times to thousands of investors in dozens of countries. But it is also my story, including a number of personal anecdotes. I hope it will be an entertaining read. Oh, and don't be surprised if you become a different kind of investor... Just smile and wonder!

Pim van Vliet, PhD

Rotterdam, the Netherlands

My home country is one of the richest and happiest places in the world. However, one disadvantage of being Dutch is that our names are often difficult to pronounce. My name is pronounced something like 'FAN FLEET'. The main advantage of being Dutch is that our nation is built on commerce and, as a result, we speak many languages and understand different cultures. I hope this book benefits from this Dutch heritage and that it will inspire investors around the globe.

Chapter One

The Opposite of What You're Aiming For

IN OUR EARLIEST YEARS MOST OF US LEARN that if you want to be successful you have to make an effort. Whether it's good exam results at high school, winning a game of football, or perhaps losing weight, we have to work to achieve it. And most of the time, this sound principle of 'sowing the seeds to reap the rewards' holds true.

But how much effort do you really need to put in to reap those rewards? Many people believe there is a positive relationship between the amount of effort you put into something and the likelihood that you will succeed. The more effort you put in, the more likely you are to succeed. But is this true?

It is not. There is something known as the law of diminishing returns. Let me clarify by applying this law to sports. You need to train if you play professional football or want to run a marathon. You really need to kick a ball or put on your running shoes a few times a week in order to develop some muscle strength. But the first 100 hours of training will have more effect than the next 100 hours and so on. Perhaps you recognize this effect, as it also might explain why it is often fun to learn new things. The learning curve is quite steep at the beginning and then it starts to gradually level off. It's the theory of diminishing returns put into practice.

Moreover, once you have put a certain amount of effort into something, any additional extra effort can paradoxically result in the opposite of what you were aiming to achieve. For example, if you train too much and fail to rest at regular intervals, it can even be damaging. The opposite of what you were aiming for (finishing that marathon) might occur: an injury might even prevent you from showing up at the start of the game or the race in the first place. Too much of something, even a good thing, can have a negative effect.

Take the amount of salt you use when preparing a dish. A little bit of salt can add flavor to the food; too much might spoil it. Vitamins are healthy, but become toxic when consumed in large quantities. And some advice for bachelors who are desperately looking for a spouse: yes, you should make the first move to approach someone you like, but too much attention might have the opposite effect and scare her (or him!) off. Losing weight? Might sound like a good plan if you need to shed a few extra pounds, but not when too much dieting results in anorexia. Studying really hard just before your exams and then showing up completely exhausted before the test itself is another example.[1] Needless to say, a good night's sleep before an exam will serve you better than studying all night long. Too much of something often causes more harm than good.

In life you should try to find the optimum between too little and too much. You need practical wisdom to determine where this

---

[1] I've witnessed this counterproductive behavior at universities in the US, Sweden, and the Netherlands.

'golden mean' is. Aristotle, a Greek philosopher, wrote extensively about the golden mean. This is the desirable middle between two extremes, one of excess and one of deficiency. The golden mean is *not* the exact middle, as this will vary according to the situation. It requires practical wisdom to find it. The Chinese philosopher Confucius also taught the doctrine of the middle way, while references to the golden mean can also be found in Buddhism, Judaism, Christianity, and in Islam.

So why this golden mean? Why am I bringing up these old philosophers? Why this focus on the fact that too much of something can result in the opposite effect to the one desired? Well, I wanted to make you familiar with the concept of a paradox. A paradox is anything that is apparently – in itself – contradictory in nature. Chances are that you are already familiar with the word, as we use it in everyday communication to express astonishment or disbelief about something that is unusual or unexpected. Paradoxes also exist in the world of investing. In fact, as a student I hit upon perhaps the biggest paradox in the investment world: low-risk stocks deliver high returns while high-risk stocks deliver low returns. Quite a surprising and remarkable finding.

Let me explain why this is remarkable. Think about the following common 'investment wisdom': the more risk you take, the better your returns will be. Most equity investors, whether they are professional money managers, such as investment advisors or hedge fund managers, or 'do-it-yourself' private investors, believe that concept of more risk, more return. But is this really true?

A lot of these investors 'aim for the moon' when it comes to managing money for their investment portfolios. They try to find the next potential Apple, Google, or Tesla. Investing in these kinds of exciting stocks is risky, as you might lose your initial investment if your potential 'super stock' turns out to be not quite so super, and perhaps even files for bankruptcy.

But what if you were to succeed in finding the next Google or Tesla in time and the stock quadrupled in price? Oh yes, then you would be laughing all the way to the bank, knowing that you'd won the jackpot and reached the moon! And what about the less exciting stocks? Well, according to many investors, boring stocks won't get you very far in life. After all, doesn't low risk equal low return? Do you know anybody who got rich quickly by investing in a slow-moving low-risk stock?

So if I tell you that low-risk stocks can make you rich while high-risk stocks can make you poor, I completely understand that your initial response might be something like: *What has the guy who came up with that statement been smoking?* I can't blame you for having those thoughts. After all, I was born and raised in the Netherlands and still live here. This statement is counterintuitive to anyone familiar with the general investment wisdom 'more risk equals more return'. So if you buy a book about investing and read in the first chapter the exact opposite to this widely accepted premise, you would be justified in questioning the author's credibility.

And, to be honest I was a bit puzzled as well when I first read about this investment paradox. Back in the days when I was an undergraduate student, I stumbled upon an academic article that described this risk–return paradox for the first time. Afterwards, as a PhD student I had plenty of time to reread and digest this fascinating study published in the early 1970s. As a result of doing this, something I will describe briefly in the following chapters, I was able to find more data to confirm that low-risk stocks beat high-risk stocks. After I received my doctorate degree I decided it was about time to put this well-tested theory into practice. Would an investment strategy based on this paradox also play out in the real world?

Well, it did! After my university years I joined an international investment management company, which manages money for institutional investors (like insurance companies, endowments, and pension funds) and private investors. Robeco is a prudent investment firm that employs many smart researchers and has a research heritage going back to the 1920s. Although it was not my original intention to start a new fund, we started a low-risk equity fund in 2006, two years after I joined the firm.

What struck me during my first months at Robeco was how the concept of risk was turned upside down in the investment industry. I had studied risk for many years at university, but in the industry, risk was not defined as losing money, but as underperforming a benchmark. I started to realize that this perspective on risk is wrong, but that it could also explain the investment paradox. I also felt that we had to do something about this and convince our existing and potential clients about this misperception of risk. And of course we also explained how they could profit from it. We managed to convince a lot of investors and the once-small fund became a strategy with over USD 15 billion worth of assets which we manage for investors from all over the world.

You might wonder why I decided to share this investment paradox with you. Because, after all, I could just focus on managing the funds and playing golf in my spare time. Well, first of all, I wanted to reach out to those who are not experts in finance. I have written many articles in several journals; I know that reading an academic paper is not something a lot of investors like to do in their spare time. So writing this easy-to-read book gives me the opportunity to explain some fascinating academic results to a broader audience. Second, I enjoy trying to explain something complex in a simple way. Simplifying is quite difficult; it's much easier to make things complicated. Third, I like to link ancient wisdom and classical virtues to the modern world of investing. Throughout my life I have discovered that moral philosophy, which teaches us how to live a good life, can be surprisingly useful when it comes to investing.

A book is a much better medium for telling this story than an academic article. The final reason why I took this challenge is because this book will save me time. When people ask about my job and what a fund manager does, I can simply refer them to this book. So, for all these reasons I want to spread the word, to show that, in order to make a good investment return, you can simply buy low-risk stocks and stay away from high-risk stocks. Oh, and I don't play golf either...

I am assuming that I haven't convinced you yet. In fact, I would be quite surprised if, at this stage, you already believed that low-risk stocks will give you high returns. A skeptical attitude helps to increase knowledge on any topic, and you need a doubting mind to challenge conventional wisdom. Bertrand Russell, a British philosopher, noted that the main problem in the world is that fools and fanatics are always so sure of themselves, while wise men are full of doubts. Therefore, I will give you plenty of evidence in this book for the existence of this investment paradox. And don't worry, it will be an easy read. In the next chapter, I'll start by sharing my first experience of the stock market with you.

Mr Thrifty Enters
the Stock Market

MR THRIFTY. If you were to ask people close to me during my childhood to describe me, this would probably be their answer. I was raised in a large Christian family in the Dutch countryside. Yes, we had tulips in our garden, but we hardly ever wore the clogs that fill most tourist shops in Amsterdam. Apart from these stereotypes my family was truly Dutch: savvy and willing to do business. My father, who was a co-owner of a family-run electronics store in our village, taught us that first you need to work hard for your money and then you need to carefully look after what you have earned.

Well, believe me, I learned that lesson... How happy I was with the little pocket money I earned by working in the family store or doing jobs around the house. Almost every day I checked my savings and searched for ways to fatten my piggy bank. Besides trying to increase my income I also focused on cost cutting: the less money I spent, the more I would have. So I put myself on a financial diet and tried not only to save as much as I could, but also to be patient and let the magic happen. But what exactly was the magic?

Early in life my father taught me another valuable lesson about the eighth wonder of the world, at least according to Albert Einstein. And no, I am not referring to his famous theory of relativity, but the 'magic' of compounding interest. The math behind it is simple (otherwise I would never have been able to grasp it at such a young age): if you put 100 dollars in a bank account, yielding 10% per year, you end up with 10 dollars of interest at the end of the first year. However, in the second year, this combined sum of 110 dollars doesn't generate 120 dollars, but 121 dollars (10% interest on 110 dollars gives a return in the second year of 11 dollars) ... Or, in other words (according to my boyhood reasoning): the magic of compounding would give me one free dollar in the second year. For a kid that was saving pennies on a daily basis, this 'eighth world wonder' seemed to be pure magic.

One day, when I was 14 years old, I found an opportunity to let my money grow at a faster pace. Back in those days, in the early 1990s, interest rates were – by today's standards – relatively high. My little treasure trove was yielding a whopping 6% per year. My father told me he had invested some money in a low-risk fixed income fund, which yielded 8% per year. I was sold, because it meant I would receive two extra guilders (NLG) for every NLG 100 I put into this fund.[1] I slaughtered my piggybank (not literally) and put most of my savings in the fund. Then, on a daily basis I followed its price movements in the newspaper and on Teletext.[2] But it was so boring! The daily price of the fund hardly fluctuated and

---

[1] The Dutch guilder was the currency of the Netherlands from 1378 to 2002, when it was replaced by the euro.

[2] Teletext was a text-based information system dating from the 1970s that was available on many TV sets in Europe. See also Wikipedia: https://en.wikipedia.org/wiki/Electra_(teletext).

if it did, it only moved by about 10 cents. After two years I couldn't stomach it anymore. I impatiently decided to remove my money from the boring bond mutual fund and directly invest it in exciting companies with high upside potential. I believed I needed to be in the stock market instead of the bond market.

My local bank advisor understood my impatience and advised me to invest in either a balanced fund or an equity fund. However, I did not like this idea for two reasons. First, I wanted to pick stocks myself as I believed I might be quite good at it and I would learn along the way. Second, I did not believe in diversification because this would limit my upside potential. Third, investing in individual stocks is far more exciting for a teenager.

One of the first companies I invested in was a high-tech company; in fact, it was a Dutch aircraft manufacturer. Despite the appealing look of its planes, the price of its stock was not exactly trading in the stratosphere. Quite the opposite. As the demand for these planes was cyclical and the production costs were too high, the company found itself in dire straits.[3] The turbulence that hit this company's balance sheet eventually caused its stock price to plummet to very low levels.

It first appeared on my radar screen during the spring of 1994. In those days the company was a renowned and well-respected producer of high-quality medium-sized airplanes, which were being sold to airlines all over the world. In 1992, part of it was bought by DASA, a German aerospace conglomerate (the precursor of EADS, the producer of the Airbus). Although the Dutch aircraft producer was facing some fierce headwinds, its German CEO reassured the employees and shareholders that they shouldn't worry about the distressing situation facing the Dutch aircraft company. Quite the contrary: during a press conference he reassured those

---

[3] Management blamed the strong German D-Mark for the high production costs, as the Dutch currency was pegged to the German D-Mark.

present in his strongly accented English that this company was his 'love baby' and would even receive extra care.

And there I was: faced with the decision of investing in this piece of Dutch aviation heritage or letting the opportunity pass. Although investors were having a bumpy ride as a result of big daily stock-price fluctuations and the company's financially distressed situation, I decided to take a 'stake' in the company and bought a large number of shares worth NLG 12 (about USD 7) each. As I was convinced that the Germans would never abandon their Dutch 'love baby', I expected that sooner or later the company would become profitable again and that its share price would shoot back up into the stratosphere.

Every day I checked the stock price movements, scanning the newspaper for any company updates in order to see how my troubled baby was doing. However, checking the daily closing price and reading the headlines soon became a pretty horrendous task. The company wasn't rising like a phoenix from the ashes and heading back into the stratosphere; in fact, the stock price took a further nose-dive over the course of the year. When the stock hit NLG 4 I couldn't handle the daily horror anymore and decided to bail out by selling all my shares. Two weeks later the shares of the company crashed when the company declared itself bankrupt. The stock kept on trading for two more years at around NLG 1 before it ceased to exist altogether. Would you like to know the name of the company? The name says it all, it was Fokker. What's in a name…

Despite having bailed out at NLG 4, I saw a large part of my savings disappear. But, in retrospect, this sad experience was perhaps one of the best things that could have happened to me. Why? Because it taught me several things an investor cannot learn at any school.

The money I lost on the stock market was worth every penny. It was the 'tuition fee' I had to pay in order to become a good investor. As I made this investment mistake early on in my life, the costs were quite limited (although huge to me at the time), while the experience would last a lifetime. Some of the things I learned from this experience:

First, don't be overconfident. The advice of the investment advisor to diversify my investments by investing in a mutual fund was prudent and wise. Simply putting all your eggs in one basket isn't a sensible thing to do, as a famous Nobel Prize winner already proved long ago.[4] However, as a teenager I believed that I would be able to outsmart other (probably more experienced) investors. This tendency or bias of individuals to be too confident is one of the most robust biases relating to human decision making documented in academic literature.[5]

Actually, the tendency among human beings to be too confident relates to another kind of bias: the optimism bias. According to academic literature, people who 'suffer' from this bias tend to look mostly on the bright side of life. I say 'suffer' as this bias actually doesn't really do any harm and actually often helps you in life.[6] Being an optimist makes you happier in general and has a positive influence on your health. But does it make you a better investor? No, it doesn't. As we have seen, looking on the bright side of a failing aircraft manufacturer's life might have prevented me from worrying too much about its future prospects, but it wasn't very beneficial to the overall value of my investment.

So, should you act like an investor who's constantly insecure about his own skills and who doubts every investment decision?

---

[4] Harry Markowitz won the Nobel Prize for economics in 1990. Portfolio Selection was his seminal paper on risk and diversification which was published in the 1952 issue of the *Journal of Finance*.

[5] James Montier has written several books on behavioral finance describing all investment biases, including overconfidence. A good and easy read is Montier's *The Little Book of Behavioral Investing*.

[6] Professor Daniel Kahneman, a psychologist who won the Nobel Prize for economics in 2002, once remarked that of all biases, optimism is often a force for good, keeping you healthy and resilient.

No, that's not the way to go forward either. In order to make the decision to buy the stock of a specific company, select a mutual fund, or enter the broad stock market you need to have at least some confidence in the quality of your investment skills. A lack of confidence could paralyze you and being overconfident is dangerous. Something in between the two is what you need – neither too much nor too little.

Second, the power of compounding is generally a force for good, but it cuts both ways. Think about it: if you lose 50% of your capital in one single transaction, you need to double your remaining capital just to break even. The stock price of my former 'love baby' Fokker fell from NLG 12 to NLG 4, a return of minus 67%. Given that the compounding then worked against me, I needed to make at least 200% in order to break even. If I had put the proceeds of what was left from my aircraft adventure into a broadly diversified mutual fund, it would have taken me ages to break even again. You can imagine that, as a teenager, I felt stuck in this situation and that my initial thought was to take on more risk in order to compensate for my losses. Selling at NLG 4 might seem painful, but if I had been forced to sell the stock at NLG 2 it would have meant that I needed investment gains of 500% in order to reach my break-even point. That would have been an even more daunting challenge. You may think that the premise of 'winning by not losing' sounds like a paradox, but it certainly holds true when investing in stocks.

Third, and most importantly, I personally experienced that high-risk investing does not automatically lead to high returns. Actually, I confused risk with return. The exciting daily volatility of the stock price, the financial distress, and the seemingly temporary decline in this airline's business momentum all looked like opportunities to me.

Somehow I seemed to be attracted to the risk of investing in this particular stock. But why? I guess my first aim was to make some money. But other motives probably also played a role. After all, it would have been a great story if things had worked out well and the price had returned to NLG 30 (not an unusual level for this stock, as it traded there in the early 1990s). Generating a return of 200% or more is a very nice story for a young kid. Also, the idea of outsmarting the rest of the market and dwarfing the returns of most other investors was very appealing to a competitive guy like me. I had also deluded myself that I was not really risking my money since I would not need it in the near future. As my investment horizon was long, I had simply convinced myself that there wouldn't be any risk. If the company was in trouble for some years to come I wouldn't care that much, as long as it prospered at some point in the future with me onboard as an investor. And last but not least, don't big returns require big risks? Within this logical framework, it's not difficult to understand that I went for the most exciting investment opportunity available on the Dutch stock market in 1994. Figure 2.1 summarizes my first experience on the stock market.

FIGURE 2.1   Stock price movement of Fokker NV over the period 1989–1997

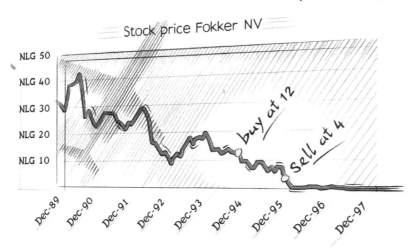

Chapter Three

The Tortoise Beats the Hare

STUPID ME. I should never have abandoned my low-risk fixed-income fund for an equity investment in a single stock called Fokker. It would have given me a healthy and wealthy return of at least 8% per year. I would probably also have had a far smoother ride, as the daily volatility of that fund was quite low. Instead, my first equity investment turned out to be a very expensive and very bumpy ride.

Bumpy, as the stock price of Fokker NV was quite volatile in the two years that I flew with this aircraft maker. Before I boarded Fokker in 1994, the stock price already had a 'reputation' for subjecting its investors to lots of turbulence. As Figure 2.1 shows, monthly price fluctuations of over 20% were common back in those days. Just to give you an example, in 1989 the price moved up from NLG 22 to over NLG 30 in just a few months. After this steep climb the shares tumbled over 30% before bottoming out back down at NLG 20. This rollercoaster ride repeated itself all the way down until the company defaulted. Fokker was a great example of a high-risk stock.

But what exactly is a high-risk stock? Is a stock risky if the company's future prospects are highly uncertain? Yes. Does risk equal uncertainty? No. Risk is uncertainty put into a number and quantifies some scenarios which might happen in the future. Elroy Dimson, a financial professor at London Business School, says risk means that more things can happen than will happen.

In the context of investments, risk applies to the potential negative scenarios in which some or all capital is lost. The *volatility* of an investment is a simple and powerful indicator of financial risk, as it measures the price fluctuations of that investment in a standardized way.[1] Volatility is quite persistent over time.[2] In other words, a stock that displays a low degree of volatility will probably also remain a low-volatility stock in the future. The same applies to high-volatility stocks.

Fokker was a prime example of a high volatility stock, as the rollercoaster ride repeated itself all the way down until the company defaulted. With hindsight, Fokker's high volatility was a good indicator of its future uncertainty and risk. If only I had known that volatility is one of the best predictors of bankruptcy, I would never have bought those shares as a teenager in the first place.

The risk of a whole range of investments or asset classes like bonds, equities, or real estate can be assessed by measuring the volatility of their returns. Given the fact that volatility is a

---

[1] Uncertainty, risk, and volatility are not the same. In 1921 economist Frank Knight wrote that risk can be measured and uncertainty cannot. Peter Bernstein has written a historical account of risk in his popular book *Against the Gods*. Nassim Taleb elaborated on this and introduced the 'Black Swan' concept in which unexpected events often have huge impact. Taleb is skeptical of relying too heavily on statistical risk measures, such as volatility, and relates this to the financial crisis. He is probably right: too much reliance on statistical risk measures can cause more harm than good.

[2] A Nobel Prize in economics was awarded to professors Robert Engle and Clive Granger in 2003 for their work on demonstrating this.

standardized indicator of financial risk, you can compare the volatility of a fixed-income fund (probably low) with the volatility of a balanced fund (probably higher) or the volatility of an equity fund (probably the highest of all).

But you can also compare the riskiness of each individual investment within an asset class. For example, you can measure the risk associated with each and every stock traded on the US stock market by measuring their historical return volatility. This might sound complicated and time consuming, but all it takes is a simple spreadsheet program (e.g. Microsoft Excel) and the closing prices of the stocks you want to compare. The spreadsheet program will calculate the amount of risk associated with each stock as measured by its historical volatility. After assessing the risks of each individual stock, you can rank them from very low risk to very high risk.

My personal investment experience with Fokker was just one anecdote. You might think right now: "*OK, too bad for you, but isn't that just one rotten apple spoiling the barrel? Can you really draw conclusions based on just one observation? Maybe you should have bought more risky Fokker-like stocks and built a broadly diversified portfolio?*" Before answering this, I would like to ask you a question: How can we figure out whether we should construct a low-risk or high-risk portfolio of stocks?

Let me give you some help. Basically there are two approaches you can use to figure out which group of stocks (low risk or high risk) provides the best returns. The first approach is a 'do-it-yourself-approach' of calculating and studying vast amounts of historical stock market data. Based on your findings, you can come up with a basic theory that describes the relationships between all the data you've studied. The second approach works the other way around. You start with an existing well-known theory about a specific subject and use this to decide which stocks to buy. In other words, you go from theory to practice.

You might wonder which approach is best: the 'practical' do-it-yourself approach or the 'theoretical' approach. As more than one road leads to Rome, perhaps both approaches give you the right answer. In fact, you may expect all theoretical approaches to be so well researched and tested by serious academics that if you were to start calculating the data yourself (with a little help from your spreadsheet) you would probably end up with the same results. At least, that's what you would expect, isn't it?

Let's start with the 'do-it-yourself' approach. In fact, because I have already performed these calculations many times in my career and you might prefer not to spend your time data crunching, it might be better to call it the 'why-don't-*you*-do-it-for me?' approach! That's fine by me, so let me tell you how I crunched the numbers before I show you the results.

So, where to start? First of all, in order to get any reliable results to draw conclusions from, you need to have reliable data. For this analysis I relied upon a pretty cool dataset, as it contains all the monthly closing prices of US traded stocks from January 1926 to December 2014. In other words, in order to investigate whether we should buy low-risk or high-risk stocks, we can research data that covers a period of more than 80 years. Don't underestimate the power of such a long time period. It gives us the opportunity to test how these groups of stocks performed during the Great Depression of the thirties, World War II, the fifties and swinging sixties as well as during multiple recessions and market booms like the Dotcom bubble in the nineties.

In fact, having a dataset that goes back more than ten years gives us lots and lots of statistical power: any results we obtain are very unlikely to be the result of pure luck or temporary effects that might disappear at some point in the future. So these observations will be robust. I dare to go even one step further. You may question any investor who claims to have found some kind of special investment method or systematic strategy based on data that do not span at least a couple of decades... I am not saying that such results are necessarily false or wrong, but when it comes to datasets and look-back periods, 'bigger and longer' really are better.

Having an extensive dataset is nice, but building low-risk or high-risk stock portfolios in an intuitive and realistic manner is even nicer. But where should we start? Let's first deal with the number of stocks.

To keep things simple, I have decided to focus on the 1,000 largest companies by market capitalization and excluded penny stocks (common shares of small public companies that trade at low prices per share, i.e. less than USD 1). By focusing on only the largest 1,000 stocks at any given moment in time, we ensure that we don't end up buying small, illiquid stocks at any point in time. For example, during the last month (December 2014) in our analysis, the 'smallest' company within our dataset had a market capitalization of USD 6 billion.

For each of these 1,000 stocks I measured the historical monthly return volatility over the past three years. So, 'on' 1 January 1929, I calculated the historical volatility of each of these 1,000 stocks for the January 1926–December 1928 period. 'On' New Year's Day 1929, I was not only able to calculate each company's risk by measuring its volatility, I could also rank all these companies in terms of their risk. And so I did just that (at my computer in 2015...). After I had ranked all these companies I created two portfolios in the simplest way you could possibly imagine: one containing the 100 stocks with the lowest risk (the low-volatility portfolio) and the other made up of the 100 riskiest stocks (the high-volatility portfolio).

In a nutshell, I focused on the 1,000 largest companies listed on the US stock market by measuring their historical volatility, ranking them from low risk to high risk and then created two portfolios. So, what's next?

Well, people normally construct stock portfolios in order to generate returns, and our goal with these portfolios is exactly the same. The two portfolios that I created 'on' New Year's Day 1929 will generate returns as long as we don't sell the stocks. And we can measure their returns to find out which one performs best. But we frequently need to check whether the individual stocks in the two portfolios still belong there. Let me clarify.

We bought the stocks because they happened to have the lowest or highest historical volatility of all the 1,000 stocks that we ranked at that particular moment in time. Although risk is quite persistent over time, a low-volatility stock can become a higher volatility stock and vice versa. That's why we select 100 stocks rather than one single stock. Sometimes this change happens gradually, sometimes it happens quickly because a low-volatility stock can also become distressed, its company accused of fraud, etc. As a consequence, you frequently need to rebalance both portfolios to ensure that they continue to contain the 100 stocks with the lowest or highest volatility at any given time. In my calculations and simulations, I took this into account and rebalanced the portfolio every quarter. If a stock in one of the portfolios no longer qualified to be there, I just sold that position and replaced it with a new stock.

Curious about the results of this endeavor? Was Fokker just a bad example? Do 100 high-risk stocks give high returns and do 100 low-risk stocks give low returns? Well…and let's have a drum roll, please…

The graph in Figure 3.1 shows the movements of both portfolios, assuming that we put USD 100 into both of them on New Year's Day 1929 and reinvested any capital gains for 86 years until New Year's Day 2015.

So, the results show that… Wait! Just stop a minute and take a very deep breath… The 'winning' portfolio is the low-volatility

FIGURE 3.1   Low-volatility stocks beat high-volatility stocks by a factor of 18

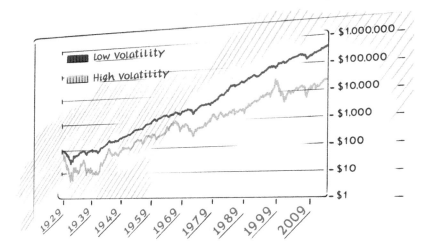

portfolio with USD 395,000, while the high-volatility portfolio's final value is only USD 21,000.

Now take a closer look at this graph. It's OK to say it out loud. And no, I haven't switched the labels and you haven't gone mad. Over this 86-year period, low-risk stocks gave an average annual return of 10.2% while for high-risk stocks this figure was only 6.4%. I do realize this might be rather puzzling for you, as this picture basically bashes all your preconceptions. It bashes everything you learn when you read a financial textbook, pursue a basic finance course, or even when you write a dissertation on risk and return (which I did). We are taught to believe that high risk gives high returns. It proves that our popular notion of risk and return in investing is totally wrong. Quite a paradox, isn't it?

In fact, it is so puzzling that academics have a scientific word for this phenomenon: anomaly. A French word to convey our absolute astonishment over this empirical fact: high-risk stocks generate *lower* returns, while it 'should' be the other way around, according to all those textbooks. Maybe we should change our theory? It's all very confusing.

The difference of 3.8% in the annual returns (with a lower volatility) means that USD 100 does not grow to USD 21,000 but to USD 395,000 over this 86-year period. Low-risk stocks make you much richer than high-risk stocks. To be precise, they would have made you more than 18 times richer. I told you, compounding is magic!

The low-volatility portfolio clearly outperformed the high-volatility portfolio and offered you a smooth 'ride to riches' at the same time, whereas the high-volatility portfolio was the rollercoaster. During the Great Depression of the 1930s, you would almost certainly have been depressed, as your initial USD 100 lost more than 90% during the stock market crash. And if you had managed to survive that emotionally, there were more fierce headwinds during the bear market of the 1970s, with losses amounting to almost 80%. During the aftermath of the Dotcom bubble? A different era, but almost the same result: a loss of over 80%. Given these figures, the high-volatility portfolio would have caused plenty of high blood pressure and sleepless nights...

What the graph in Figure 3.1 actually shows is that the low-volatility portfolio wins by losing less during times of stress. A skeptical person – and I hope you are one – might argue that it makes a lot of sense that the low-volatility portfolio outperforms the high-volatility portfolio if you start measuring performance from just before the Great Depression. I agree with that person. After all, the high-volatility portfolio would only be worth a little over USD 5 when the market bottomed out during the spring of 1932, while the low-volatility portfolio would still be worth over USD 30. However, it was not just the 1929–1932 crash that caused the low-volatility portfolio to finish ahead. If we were to start both portfolios in the spring of 1932, the low-volatility portfolio would still 'win' by a very significant margin.

Although the results of our 'practical' approach are quite promising, we've got ourselves a problem here. Indeed, a problem or, for some, an inconvenient truth. The problem is that our results cannot be true according to the 'theoretical' approach and conventional investor wisdom. Despite the empirical proof that low-volatility investing performs better than high-volatility investing, most people still want to believe that high-risk stocks yield higher returns than low-risk stocks.

Buying the most risky stocks does not give you the highest return; in fact, it seems to be the other way around. Chapter 16 shows that this investment paradox can be found almost everywhere you look, which will really make you wonder. But what should we do with the counterintuitive finding that high risk gives low returns and low risk gives high returns? Should we change the theory so it fits the data, or should we change the data to confirm the theory? Well, as we cannot rewrite history or historical price movements, it's probably best to change the theory. However, changing the perceived relationship between risk and return for every investor in the world is quite challenging, as we will need to convince a lot of people.

Maybe a story will help. Some of you know the fable of the tortoise and the hare. The tortoise moves slowly and steadily, while the hare is fast but takes a nap along the way and ends up being beaten by the tortoise. Not the outcome you would expect. Figure 3.2 illustrates that slow and steady beats fast and volatile. This old story demonstrates how the virtue of persistence beats the vice of overconfidence.

The steady 'tortoise stocks' beat the fast 'hare stocks'.[3] The moral of our story? Never underestimate the proof of empirical evidence over a compelling theory. And this won't be the last time we come across the hare and the tortoise in this book…

FIGURE 3.2   The tortoise beats the hare

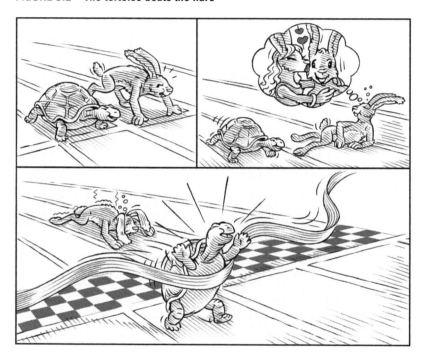

---

[3] The Greeks also philosophized about a tortoise race. In one story, a tortoise convinces Achilles that he will win a race if he just gets a head start of, say, 100 meters. The tortoise uses a paradox and argues that the quickest runner can never overtake the slowest, since the pursuer must first reach the point from which the pursued started, so the pursued will always maintain a lead despite the fact that he is slower. This is Zeno's paradox on infinite distance.

Chapter Four

A Little Bit Is Enough

YOU HAVE JUST SEEN THE INVESTMENT PARADOX IN ACTION: low-risk stocks beating high-risk stocks. Deep historical analysis demonstrates that investing in a low-volatility portfolio delivers a far better result (up to 20 times) than investing in a high-volatility portfolio. Oh, and let's not forget: this low-risk portfolio even lets you sleep at night, given the fact that the higher return comes with a lower amount of risk. It seems almost too good to be true, doesn't it? Especially as it defies the well-known theoretical relationship between risk and return.

Does this mean that you should now immediately delete that part of your investment brain and replace it with this new risk–return insight, based on a single graph showing two portfolios? Better not. Although I am quite sure that you'll have a different view on risk and return by the time you finish this book, it's probably best to first critically assess (a more gentle alternative to 'bash') these findings extensively before you do so. So let's focus again on the evidence presented in the previous chapter.

The two portfolios that we looked at were quite different with regards to the amount of risk and return they delivered over the course of 86 years. The low-volatility portfolio yielded 10.2% per year whereas the high-volatility portfolio provided an annual return of 6.4% per year. So far we haven't quantified the level of each portfolio's volatility, but just referred to them as being either low risk or high risk. So here you go: the annualized volatility of the low-risk portfolio was 13% whereas the high-risk portfolio had a volatility of 36%.[1] So, about 2.5 times riskier. In order to put these numbers into perspective, I have shown these data points on the graph in Figure 4.1.

Besides displaying the risk and return of these two portfolios, the graph also highlights the actual relationship between risk and return, shown by the line. Given the fact that the high-volatility portfolio has a lower return than the low-volatility portfolio, our results indicate a negative (!) relationship between risk and return. The tortoise beats the hare.

FIGURE 4.1   High-risk portfolio generates lower returns

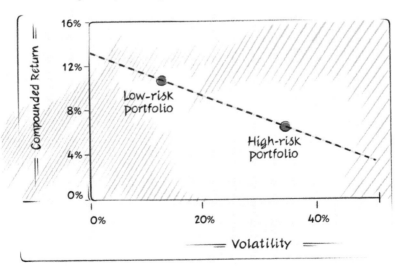

---

[1] Volatility is the degree of price variation. As a rule of thumb, 20% is the average annual volatility of an average stock. A typical stock has a 1/3 chance of going up or down by more than 20% in the course of a year and has a 2/3 chance of staying within this 20% bandwidth.

But let's be a bit skeptical at this point. To what extent can we *really* say that the relationship between risk and return is inverted, given the fact that we only considered the 100 most volatile stocks and the 100 least volatile stocks? Perhaps these two extreme portfolios are just an exception to this rule? Maybe there is a positive relationship between risk and return, in the sense that buying more volatile stocks will deliver higher returns, but that this rule just doesn't apply to the 100 most risky (that is, most volatile) stocks in the investment universe.

Just do the math: if the high-risk portfolio contains a lot of 'Fokker-like' stocks (stocks that go bankrupt eventually), it should not come as a big surprise to you that the overall return of that highly volatile portfolio is being hurt by the defaults of some of these extremely volatile stocks.

In order to investigate whether our two portfolios are, in themselves, an exception to the general rule of return being positively related to risk, I created eight other portfolios. I just divided the 1,000 largest stocks into ten groups, ranked according to volatility, each containing 100 stocks. Again, each of these investment portfolios started life on New Year's Day, 1929.

Are you curious about the results? Well, just take a look at the graph in Figure 4.2. It shows the risk and return for each of the ten portfolios. The line shows the actual relationship between risk and return.

As you can see, it's not positive, but it's not negative either. The line rises slightly, before falling sharply. The inverse relationship between risk and return is not just because the portfolio with the highest volatility delivers a mediocre return. Not at all in fact! Most high-risk portfolios, portfolios 8 and 9 too, generate returns that are lower than those of most low-risk portfolios. Although each of these portfolios exposes you to a higher degree of volatility, they fail to give you an extra reward for this higher risk. Quite the reverse, in fact: they generate lower returns. More risk *and* less return. Ouch, painful.

FIGURE 4.2   Taking on some risk pays off, but too much risk results in low returns

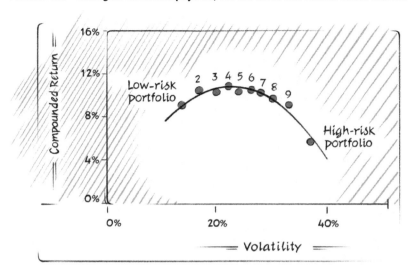

Still, some portfolios seem to adhere to the rule of 'more risk equals higher returns'. For instance, if you hadn't bought the 100 stocks with lowest volatility, but had instead bought the portfolio with a little more volatility (portfolio 2), you would have earned a little over 11% per year, compared to the 10.2% return of the lowest risk portfolio. And if you were willing to take on even more risk by buying portfolio 4, you would have earned as much as 12% per year. The golden mean becomes visible in Figure 4.2: a little bit of risk can provide additional return, but don't overshoot. I've used the metaphor of salt before; a little bit adds some flavor, but too much will spoil your meal. Figure 4.3 illustrates this vividly. The same applies to risk. Taking some risk increases your average return, but too much will spoil it.

And the graph confirms the existence of the investment paradox. As I explained in the first chapter, a paradox is something that's seemingly contradictory. People tend to believe relationships are straightforward or linear, because that is a simple rule of thumb, but in this case it is clearly not a straight upward-sloping line. At first the relationship is slightly positive, but then it levels off before quickly turning negative.

FIGURE 4.3   Take stock market risk like you use salt

Low-risk stocks beating high-risk stocks sounds like a para-dox to many investors, because they believe more risk should lead to better returns. It can't be true, especially for investment profes-sionals, because they have been taught exactly the opposite. Most investors have learned this from studying well-known finance text-books, attending the best universities, or listening to the smart-est professors. This makes you wonder whether these well-trained investors have been looking at the right numbers.

Chapter Five

Ignoring the Eighth Wonder of the World

IT REALLY MAKES YOU WONDER, DOESN'T IT? If a relatively simple historical simulation of ten portfolios reveals that the relationship between risk and return is exactly the opposite – or flat at best – why hasn't the modern myth of a linear and positive relationship between risk and return been 'debunked' yet by other researchers or investors? Haven't they had access to all these stock price data too?

Well, I admit that maybe not everybody has such an extensive stock market database as I do, but good databases are widely available at most universities. Did I perhaps use 'incorrect' data which caused an 'incorrect' relationship between volatility and return to appear? Nope, I can assure you that I didn't.[1]

---

[1] In 2007 we published a paper ('The Volatility Effect: Lower Risk without Lower Return') in the *Journal of Portfolio Management* on this subject. Here, we explained, the basic test in more detail using academic standards with respect to replication and empirical rigor. It earned me and my co-author David Blitz a Citation of Excellence award in 2008.

I believe it was something else that caused this evidence to be overlooked by many researchers. The proof that low-volatility stocks perform better than high-volatility stocks has been there in the data all along, especially since the quality of datasets has improved in recent years.[2] But it remained hidden from many researchers because they chose to take a short-term perspective instead of a long-term one when looking at stock returns. Let me explain this before you start to lose your focus.

All the return figures that I have shared with you so far are the investment returns that have been measured over multiple years and even multiple decades. These are the kind of returns that Albert Einstein once described as the eighth wonder of the world: compounded returns. That's right: the return figures that include the magic 'return upon return' effect.

These compounded returns are equally real for every single investor in the world – from a large collective pension fund to a teenager with a desire to buy a highly volatile aircraft manufacturer. It is the actual return that you would have made had you invested in a stock or portfolio and held on to it for a long period of time (e.g. years). For real investors, living in the real world, they are real return figures, in real dollars.

As compounded returns are the same for all investors, you might expect academic researchers to use the same numbers as investors like you and me. Indeed, you might expect them to do so. But usually they don't. They tend to focus on so-called 'single-period returns'. In most academic studies, a monthly return is all that matters and there is a reason for this monthly time horizon

---

[2] My PhD supervisor, Werner de Bondt, compared the study of risk and return with the study of happiness in marriages. "When you study that, it is also important to include the divorces in your marriage database". Interestingly, not all delistings and bankruptcies were properly included in the CRSP database until the 1990s, which gave too rosy a picture of the performance of high-risk stocks in earlier studies.

choice.[3] However, this focus on a period of a month only makes sense if your presumed investment horizon is exactly one month as well.

But how many investors really have a one-month horizon? Chances are that you have a multiple-period horizon of many quarters, years, and perhaps even decades. And even if you don't, chances are your life insurance company, your 401k, or the investment manager of your pension fund does. In other words, single-period monthly returns may be nice and handy, but most of the time they're not realistic.

To illustrate this small but important difference, let me give you an easy example. Imagine you buy the stock of a car manufacturer on New Year's Day (presuming the markets are open that day) at a price of USD 100. During the first month the stock loses 50% and during the second month it gains 50%. What would have been your investment return?

It depends on how you calculate returns. Over this time period, the price fell to USD 50 and went back up to USD 75, as shown in Figure 5.1. So you would have lost 25% of your initial investment. But if you simply average these two monthly returns, +50% and -50%, you would have had a 0% return. So you either lose 25% or break even with 0%. It's a case of compound versus simple returns. Quite a difference, isn't there?

This difference in returns is often minor, but the consequences can be major, as the previous example demonstrates. A compounded return calculates the dollar return over the entire investment period, while a simple return covers a much shorter period.

---

[3] The Nobel Prize winning Capital Asset Pricing Model (CAPM) is a very elegant model assuming a positive and linear relationship between (systematic) volatility and return. When the CAPM is tested, virtually all researchers assume the evaluation period to be no longer than one month, otherwise the statistical power would not be sufficient.

FIGURE 5.1 You lose 25% of your initial sum if you first lose 50% and then gain 50%

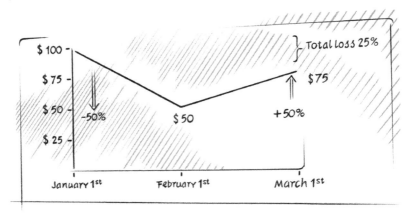

So, what would happen if we looked at the ten portfolios again and replaced the compounded returns with the simple returns assuming only a one-month horizon? Would this small difference in the method for calculating average returns have any impact on the existence of the investment paradox? Well, let's just look at the numbers in Table 5.1. The table shows the ten portfolios grouped from the lowest amount of risk (portfolio 1) up to the highest amount of risk (portfolio 10).

As you can see, the paradox becomes less clear in this table, when simple returns are used. The high-volatility portfolio 10

TABLE 5.1 The difference between simple and compounded returns increases as the level of risk increases. Note: these compounded returns are also shown in Figure 4.2

	Low risk									High risk
Portfolio	1	2	3	4	5	6	7	8	9	10
Returns										
Simple	10.6%	12.3%	12.8%	13.7%	13.6%	14.3%	14.4%	14.4%	14.6%	12.6%
Compounded	10.2%	11.6%	11.5%	12.0%	11.5%	11.7%	11.3%	10.7%	10.1%	6.4%
Difference	0.4%	0.7%	1.3%	1.7%	2.1%	2.6%	3.1%	3.7%	4.5%	6.2%

'delivers' an average simple return of 12.6% per year, whereas its compounded return is almost half of that, a mediocre 6.4%.

So, apparently the paradox of low-risk stocks making you rich and high-risk stocks making you poor does exist, although it is hidden in the shadows of statistics. It seems to be only visible to those who know where to look. In 1975, an American finance professor, Robert Haugen, knew where to look as he discovered its existence. He did so by observing the compounded returns of low-risk and high-risk investment portfolios. Again, I want to stress that most academic studies use simple returns, so Robert Haugen took a different perspective.[4] I read his work while still an undergraduate student, and to this day am surprised that his findings have been ignored by so many academics for so long.[5]

Back to compounding. Looking at the table it's clear that many investors (and academics) are not even aware of this paradox. Portfolio simulations with simple returns prevent it from showing up. Agreed, the highest risk portfolio (portfolio 10) doesn't seem to obey the wisdom of higher risk generating higher returns, but the results of portfolios 1 to 9 show that if a portfolio becomes more risky, the returns also seem to increase slightly. So, the risk–return relationship seems to be weakly positive, with just one exception. But to throw an entire theory away just because of the odd rotten apple or the observation of one single professor?[6] No, for most academics that's really a bridge too far.

---

[4] Confession time: in my own thesis on downside risk I also used simple returns and ignored the eighth world wonder of compounded returns. See also: van Vliet, P. (2004), *Downside Risk and Empirical Asset Pricing* (http://repub.eur.nl/pub/1819).

[5] By the way, if you are interested in academic studies, but are not linked to a university, I would like to refer you to a great research database called SSRN. It contains many high-quality research studies, free of charge, including several articles by Professor Haugen.

[6] This fact has only recently been acknowledged in the academic literature. Using simple returns, Ang, Hodrick, Xing, and Zhang show that stocks with high company-specific risk have low returns. This 2006 *Journal of Finance* study helped make part of the paradox more accepted among financial academics.

Still, there is more and more empirical evidence to support the paradox.[7] Not only for the US stock market as we have shown in this chapter, but also for European, Japanese, and emerging stock markets such as China, Brazil, and South Africa. The paradox is also found within every industry sector. Once you are aware of it, it pops up just about everywhere. Later on we will explore some fascinating evidence in other large markets such as the market for corporate bonds.

You might wonder: *what's in it for me as an investor?* I believe quite a lot. First of all, you've seen that high risk leads to low returns and low risk leads to high returns. Second, your investment horizon matters a lot. The longer your investment horizon, the greater the extent to which risk will hurt your long-term returns through compounding effects. For a high-risk portfolio this difference is more than 6% per year. That is really a big difference and not a small detail you can just ignore. This compounding effect explains why this paradox has not been on the radar of most financial researchers.

Although the results in this chapter prove the existence of the investment paradox, one big question remains unanswered: WHY do low-risk stocks beat high-risk stocks? This is an important question; one I have asked myself many, many times for about half of my life now. Why do these low-risk stocks do so well in the long run? Is it because they have a secret business model that helps them to deliver high returns? Or does it have something to do with the people who shun these steady stocks? Or is it something else? It's time to answer some questions. Hold on to your skepticism and let's hop to the next chapter!

---

[7] In their 2014 study, Frazzini and Pederson scale low-risk stocks up and scale high-risk stocks down and bring them to the same risk level. This elegant approach enables a fair 'apples with apples' comparison and solves the compounding issue. Perhaps not surprisingly, the paradox then becomes very visible and significant.

Robert Haugen

1942 - 2013

The man who discovered the investment paradox;
he knew where to look in the 1970s.

Chapter Six

It's All a Matter
of Perspective

MANY INVESTORS ARE NOT AWARE of the investment paradox because they ignore the eighth wonder of the world and so fail to see its effect in the first place. But does this compounding versus simple returns perspective explain why the investment paradox exists? Is this difference in the method applied to calculating portfolio returns the sole explanation for why low-risk stocks beat high-risk stocks?

Well, in order to answer this question, let's first take a step back. The paradox also has to do with how we look at the world. Please have a look at the picture in Figure 6.1.

The picture illustrates that what you see depends on how you look at something. Depending on how you look at it, there are either three or four bars. Perhaps you first saw four and then three, or perhaps it was the other way around. Funny isn't it? It's all a matter of the perspective you choose. Because what you see ultimately depends on how you look at things.

FIGURE 6.1   It's all a matter of perspective

Having looked at this picture, let me take you back in time, to the time when I made a career switch from academia to the world of asset management. Let's go back to January 2005, when I gained a new perspective on risk.

Up to then, I had been writing my PhD thesis on – and this will not surprise you – 'the downside risk of equities'. After four years of research and teaching students I started my new career armed with a briefcase filled with 'my' investment paradox, some other anomalies, and my own investment experience (trust me, I didn't bring a scale model of a Fokker plane along with me). I started working as a researcher in the quantitative research department of an investment management firm. Now I could finally put all my relevant academic knowledge into practice.[1] In the field of quantitative finance, this really was the best place to be. Just imagine: the Netherlands is known for its vast pension funds and there are

---

[1] Karl Popper, a twentieth-century Austrian-British philosopher, stated that it is worthwhile trying to discover more of the world, even if this only teaches us how little we know. After completing my PhD thesis, I could not have agreed more with him.

plenty of highly trained financial econometricians. Combine the two and you end up with a truly innovative investment culture.

This investment department translates academic insights into profitable investment strategies for clients and analyzes which strategies will deliver the highest and most consistent returns. If, after rigorous research and historical simulations, we find a robust strategy, we can put our theory into practice.

One day I was discussing the type of research projects we conducted with my colleague David Blitz, head of quantitative equity research at Robeco. Most of the time these involved – perhaps obviously – looking for strategies that would deliver the highest returns possible. However, clients were not always prepared to give us complete freedom in how we invested. We had to come up with strategies that delivered high returns but within certain risk parameters. All pretty logical so far, isn't it? Nobody wants to recklessly take risk in pursuit of high returns.

But there was something that really struck me when I started working in the investment industry. Something I was less aware of while working at the university, but that is common among professionals in the investment industry. They have a different perspective when it comes to risk and this is caused by an almost obsessive need to benchmark the performance of investment managers. I had studied risk for many years, but quickly learned a new risk concept in my first week in asset management. It was the concept of *relative* risk.

In the previous chapters we've looked at the risk and return figures of portfolios of stocks with different levels of volatility. All the figures so far are *absolute* risk figures: stock-price fluctuations as a result of gaining and losing money. Volatility captures these fluctuations and is an absolute risk measurement.

However, many professional investors don't pay that much attention to these absolute risk numbers. They are more interested in the risk of each of these portfolios compared to the market: in having a *relative* risk perspective. For them, it is not the risk of losing money, but the risk of lagging the market. Or doing worse than their peers. For example, you might make 20% in a given year, but if the market returns 40% then this is not a good performance. And if you lose 20%? Well, that all depends on the market. If it falls 40%, your performance is quite good, but if it generates returns of 0%, your performance is quite poor. You see, investing is a relative game.

So, if your stock portfolio moves closely in line with the market, it has a low relative risk. And if the portfolio moves more independently from the market, this means a higher relative risk. This risk is as easy to calculate as volatility. You simply look at the relative price instead of the absolute price fluctuations. It is as easy as that.

The funny thing about relative volatility is that even if a stock has no risk at all, it can still be very risky on a relative basis. Let me explain.

Suppose a stock always generates gains of 10% a year, while the market varies between -40% and +60%. How risky is this stock from a relative perspective? Sometimes it lags the market by 50% and sometimes it performs 50% better than the market. From a relative risk perspective, this steady stock is very risky. From an absolute perspective, there's no risk at all because every year you earn 10% with no volatility. It's like looking at the bars in the picture. Some see three, while others see four. It is all a matter of perspective.

Professional investors have to focus on relative risk to prove to their bosses, clients, and others that their performance is above average. Remember they are not managing their own money. They are professionals and constantly have to explain their performance relative to a certain kind of yardstick or benchmark. Investment strategies are usually compared on a like-for-like basis. Institutional investors prefer to see a consistently better performance than the benchmark. This is known as outperformance and achieving a high relative return with a low relative risk is usually their sole purpose in their investment life.

The market portfolio consists of the weighted average of all stocks. It is the ultimate yardstick and most investors compare the results of their investment managers to the risks and returns of the market. The performance of the overall market (an index like the S&P 500 or MSCI World, for example) is their benchmark. And most of the time they have every reason to do this. If your portfolio generates the same returns as the market, but has a high level of relative risk, you would probably be better (and cheaper) off by just buying an index fund which just tracks the market.

What's more, as an investment professional you run an extra type of risk if you select a 'high relative risk, same return' kind of investment for your clients. This is the risk of losing your job by selecting the wrong type of stocks. This career risk is paramount. In order not to lose your job (or clients) as a professional investor, you have to make sure you select stocks that beat the market instead of giving market-like returns. So the focus is on return first and risk second.

What kind of risk? Yes, relative risk. But, let's go back to my experience of entering the world of asset management. The research department I joined had developed a stock-selection model in 1994 which aimed to deliver a high return while maintaining a low level of relative risk. This quantitative model is based on proven factors and has been used by portfolio managers since then as the basis for their investment decisions. In addition, a strategy that exclusively follows the investment signals given by this model has generated excellent real-life results since 2002.

I was happy to see that academic insights were translated into products for major professional clients. One day I brought up the subject of the investment paradox in a conversation with David. I knew he had also read Robert Haugen's research and knew that low-risk stocks gave market-like returns with lower volatility.

By then David had already been working in the investment management industry for ten years, so I wondered whether he had considered adding a low-volatility factor to the stock-selection model to enable clients to benefit from the investment paradox. Although he answered this question more than ten years ago, I can still vividly remember his emphatic and thought-provoking answer: *"Pim, if we add a low-risk factor to our existing model the relative risk would increase a lot. From our clients' perspective it is a risky strategy, without much additional return. . ."*

I was flabbergasted. There I was having just switched careers from the academic to the investment management world, with my bag full of proven academic insights, burning with ambition to turn these into investment strategies, confronted with the idea that most investors were not interested in low absolute risk portfolios. And why? Because it didn't seem to fit into their world of 'low relative risk'. Low absolute risk is considered to be high relative risk. It's a matter of perspective – quite a paradox if you ask me.

I learned quickly and started to realize that for many professional investors, a low-risk strategy is not attractive at all. Agreed, the relative risk is high. But why is relative risk so important to professional investors? Clients should only care about the real return figures, as these numbers are the only ones that really matter if you need to match an investment objective.

Quite simply, too much relative risk could be a career killer. Relative risk means that you deviate from your peers and your benchmark. Suppose you find a perfect stock with a guaranteed 10% return per year and the market goes up by 30% in one year and down by 7% the next. After two years both investments would have grown by an average compounded rate of 10%. However, in the first year you will lag the market by 20% and in the second year outperform by 17%. In the first year you won't receive any bonus and could even be fired. In the second year, if you still have your job, you will outperform by 17% but only make up your previous underperformance. So, from a relative perspective, this no-risk stock is very risky and very unattractive.

So, from the relative risk perspective of an investment professional managing his career, it makes perfect sense to pass up the opportunity of investing in a low-risk investment strategy. It's just the result of being caught in a relative risk framework.

Initially I only looked at the right (or bright!) side of Figure 6.2, but soon discovered that most professional investors only focused on the left side of the figure. By the way, here we conservatively assume that low-volatility stocks generate exactly the same returns as the market, but with *lower* absolute risk and *higher* relative risk.

David Blitz and I knew that we had to convince our potential clients that they needed to change their perspective on risk from relative to absolute. We had to change their investment paradigm. Because a low-risk portfolio only makes perfect sense if real absolute downside risk is what matters. It makes no sense if you care about relative risk. Not selecting a low-risk portfolio because it doesn't fit into a relative risk framework is kind of strange,

FIGURE 6.2   Low volatility framed in two perspectives

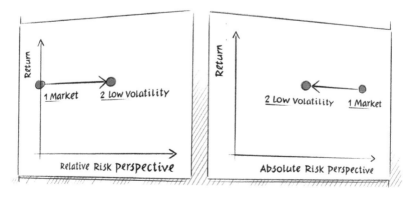

especially given the fact that the clients of these professionals will receive higher returns in the long run and face lower risks. Those poor investment professionals and their clients! The formers' worries about career risk mean the latter don't profit from this investment paradox.

But lucky you! The fact that relative risk and career risk keep professional investors away from low-risk stocks offers a great opportunity to those investors who aren't so concerned about relative risk. If the relative risk of your investment portfolio is not being closely monitored by your spouse, and your partner is unlikely to 'fire' you for buying low-risk stocks, you are in the perfect position to invest in them. It might seem to be another paradox, but private investors are far less constrained than professional investors and so better able to reap the rewards of investing in these attractive low-risk stocks. When I started developing this strategy, I actually thought it would be of most interest to clients managing their own portfolios. People like my father, who have never looked at benchmarks, but who care about increasing and protecting their capital. So, if you do not have a benchmark, lucky you!

The constraints faced by professional investors when confronted with a low-risk investment strategy might be one of the best explanations as to why investing in low-risk portfolios 'works' in the first place. If a lot of professional investors are unable to allocate funds to these kinds of portfolios, these 'underloved' strategies become 'underowned' or overlooked by other investors and so offer better returns. But there are more reasons why investors are not always attracted to low-risk stocks. Just turn the page and I'll tell you why they don't fall in love with these gems!

David Blitz

"Benchmarks can completely change our perspective on risk".

Chapter Seven

The Dark Appeal of Risk

As a child, my mother told me that comparing yourself with others can make you feel unhappy. Immanuel Kant, a nineteenth-century German philosopher, stated that jealousy and envy are destructive. Besides philosophers, all major religions warn against the negative effects of envy, jealousy, and coveting.[1] Nowadays, in the twenty-first century, real-time information is abundant and available. It has become easier and more usual to compare yourself with others. But trying to keep up with the Joneses can be quite exhausting, and even harmful as illustrated in Figure 7.1.

Eric Falkenstein is the respected author of two books on low-volatility investing in which he provides some brilliant insights into this phenomenon. He emphasizes how our human tendency to compare ourselves with others is biologically understandable. He also argues that a relative risk framework stimulates rather than

---

[1] The tenth commandment in the Bible is 'Thou shalt not covet'. In Islam and Buddhism, envy is referred to as 'hassad' and 'irshya', respectively, and not considered good. In Hinduism, envy is linked to losing personal balance.

FIGURE 7.1   Jealousy is harmful

PLEASE GOD, IF YOU CAN'T MAKE
ME THIN, MAKE MY FRIENDS FAT!

mitigates envy.[2] As envy is such a powerful emotion, we should not underestimate its influence on investment decisions.

The focus of the investment management industry on relative risk is probably not the only explanation for why low-risk stocks are overlooked by so many investors on such a massive scale.[3] Let's recap here. First, many investors *do not see* the paradox because they ignore the eighth wonder of compounding returns. Second,

---

[2] In his books, Eric Falkenstein gives numerous examples from biology (e.g. mating) to economics and argues why a relative focus is so commonly observed in nature and society throughout the ages. For example, he discusses the famous Ellsberg paradox. Western countries have grown richer, but not happier as a whole. For economists this seems strange, as utility is linked to wealth and income. Interestingly, this paradox can be understood from a relative perspective, but is puzzling from an absolute perspective.
[3] It is useful to draw fair comparisons from time to time, but we shouldn't go too far. The golden mean can also be applied to the use of peer group comparisons and relative risks.

many professional investors are *unable to apply* the paradox because of their relative risk paradigm and career constraints.

But there's also a powerful third explanation: many investors even *don't want to* buy low-risk stocks because high-risk stocks are so much more appealing to them. That's right, these low-risk stocks are usually unexciting and don't convey the idea of being investments that will make you money easily and quickly.

As I discussed earlier, investors managing their own money are not constrained by benchmarks and relative risks. Most individual investors can buy whatever stocks they like, as long as their broker has them to sell. And most of them do just that.

Individual investors tend to invest in what they perceive to be attractive. So what type of stocks are these? In reality, they tend to buy stocks as if they are lottery tickets. They seem to fall victim to the allure of volatile, sexy, and headline-grabbing stocks. One academic study even looks into the profile of investors who own the most volatile stocks. There seems to be a general preference for highly volatile, lottery-type stocks among investors with a weaker socio-economic background.[4] So, high-risk stocks are 'poor man's stocks'? Ouch – I was young and poor when I bought my first risky stock.

Stocks of companies with exciting new business models in exciting new industries are their favorites. These investors are not so concerned whether the company will be an everlasting success story, but focus more on how big their success will be and the size of the rewards for those who bought their shares. These exciting stocks make you look good to your friends and family when you tell them that you had the brilliant foresight to buy them early on.

History is abundant with these kinds of 'sexy' stocks. Take, for example, the famous South Sea Bubble that took place in

---

[4] Alok Kumar produced quite a readable study on this topic: 'Who Gambles in the Stock Market' in the *Journal of Finance* in 2009.

eighteenth-century England.[5] After the bubble burst in 1720 and having lost a fortune with this volatile stock investment, Sir Isaac Newton remarked that he could 'calculate the movement of stars, but not the madness of men'. Sadly, history tells us that not many investors have become rich by owning risky stocks.

From a business perspective, it also makes sense for mutual fund managers to keep chasing stocks with high expected returns. Because what happens when a fund manager is able to select stocks that outperform the market? Obviously the portfolio does very well and its success is noticed by those who have the job of selecting the best and brightest portfolio managers. And they recommend this star fund manager to others. The result? The manager's fund probably receives substantial sums of new money, which translates into a higher income for the asset management firm and makes his bosses happy.[6] And as a reward, they will probably give him a nice bonus.

Oh, and don't forget the analysts. Most equity analysts enter the discipline hoping to find attractive stocks as a junior analyst, become noticed after a few years, and then to become portfolio managers or star analysts. So, in order to climb up the asset management career ladder, they need to make sure their results are impressive. All they have to do is find stocks that have a relatively high potential to deliver outperformance compared to the overall market (they play the relative risk game as well). Just like fund managers, they focus on and recommend stocks that are likely to outperform the market. So they too have a clear incentive to focus on risky stocks.

---

[5] The South Sea Bubble refers to the speculative trading of shares of the South Sea Company, a company which was founded in 1711 in the United Kingdom and obtained the exclusive right – a monopoly – to trade with South America.

[6] Jason Karceski wrote an academic paper on this in 2002. Return-chasing behavior of mutual fund clients causes mutual fund managers to select high-risk stocks, 'Returns-Chasing Behavior, Mutual Funds, and Beta's Death', *Journal of Financial and Quantitative Analysis*.

So there you go. For most asset managers, fund managers, and analysts, it pays to keep on investing in high-risk stocks, although deep historical datasets prove that this is not a winners' game. I would like to emphasize that this behavior is deeply rooted, understandable, and fully rational. This is what makes it such a powerful driving force in the markets. Especially if you take into account the fact that nowadays most money is managed by professionals rather than the owners of the money themselves. This may be stating the obvious, but for people who invest their own money (people like my father), it just doesn't make any sense at all.

So these might be the reasons why low-risk stocks are overlooked in the market. First, the perspective on risk causes professional investors to chase high-risk stocks. Second, career concerns encourage professional investors to chase high-risk stocks. Third, business concerns stimulate asset management firms to sell high-risk funds. Fourth, low-risk stocks are not sexy and do not have the 'lottery-ticket' element. Virtually everybody seems to be drawn to the dark and risky side of the stock market.

At this point, you might feel like saying *"Thank you for that Mr Preacher"*, given all these reflections on the asset management industry, low-risk investing, and life in general. I don't mind, as my aim is to make sure you really understand the root of this investment paradox. Perhaps you are wondering what you can do yourself to buck this trend and not fall victim to this relative thinking.

Well, the answer is 'relatively' simple: all you need to do is change your perspective. Try to see three bars where others see four. Forget about comparing your performance with others. Just focus on absolute risk and long-term capital growth. Don't ignore the eighth wonder of the world and resist the allure of singing sirens in the form of high-risk stocks. Just buy low-risk stocks and be patient. That's all you need to do.

Eric Falkenstein

"Envy is at the root of the investment paradox".

Chapter Eight

Buy Them Cheap and Remember the Trend Is Your Friend

ALL YOU NEED ARE LOW-VOLATILITY STOCKS. Just make sure you get your hands on a basket of low-volatility stocks, buy them, keep them, but make sure you sell if another, better low-volatility stock is available.

"Woah, whoa, whoa, Mr van Vliet. . . . Not so fast! So you are now telling me all I have to do is to focus on low-volatility stocks and forget all the other investment advice? That I can just buy every low-volatility stock and not have to worry about anything else?"

If the statement 'All You Need Are Low-Volatility Stocks!' causes your mind to literally buzz with questions, that really makes my day. Questions like these are proof of a healthy skepticism. Oh, and don't worry if you haven't reached the questioning stage yet. I appreciate how patient you are being with me. But let's stay focused here: is low volatility really all that matters and can we ignore other important investment theories when constructing a low-volatility portfolio?

Yes, you really can! And if you were to do so, you'd probably see quite satisfying results, as shown in Chapter 3. But you will also forego a fortune if you ignore other valuable investment insights and focus solely on investing in low-volatility stocks, and I will show you how. It's more a case of: 'All You Need Are Low-Volatility Stocks With Two Additional Ingredients'. OK, so let's start searching for the two ingredients you need to spice up your portfolio.

But where to start? Well, let's take a step back here. Our goal is to buy low-volatility stocks, as they deliver satisfying results. But if you bought every low-volatility stock out there, your portfolio would be enormous. So you have to choose. If you could choose between two stocks with exactly the same low-risk characteristics but one was very expensive and the other was very cheap, chances are you'd opt for the cheap one.

This is the first ingredient. Because, just like a lot of other things in life, it pays to focus not only on *what* you buy, but also on the *price* you are to pay for it. This idea of buying cheap stocks is a popular and well-known investment strategy, applied by many investors all over the world. Maybe you've already heard of the concept of value investing. Over a thousand books have been written about it and many famous investors adhere to this way of investing.[1]

Although there are numerous different ways to value invest, the common denominator is to invest in stocks that are – temporarily – 'on sale'. Value investors hunt for those stocks that are – often legitimately – not in favor with other investors. Their stock prices are often cheap when compared to the company's intrinsic value

---

[1] Value investors like Warren Buffett, Walter Schloss, Mario Gabelli, Christopher Browne, and Joel Greenblatt are publicly well known. Eugene Fama, Andrei Shleifer, and Rob Arnott also promote value investing and their theories appeal to investors with an interest in academic research and evidence-based investing.

based on its fundamentals. Once they return to favor, their share prices rebound and value investors make a decent return. It's the concept of buying 1 dollar's worth of value for 60 cents and having the patience to wait for those 60 cents to bounce back to at least 1 dollar.

The famous investor Benjamin Graham is sometimes dubbed the 'founding father' of value investing, and following this line of reasoning, Warren Buffett is the equivalent of his 'son'. The superior returns generated by value investors caught the attention of the academic world and many researchers tried to establish whether it really pays off to invest in stocks with a low price relative to the value of the underlying company's fundamentals. They confirmed that cheap stocks outperformed expensive stocks in terms of a range of value characteristics. For example, they proved that it makes sense to invest in stocks with a low stock price compared to the value of the company's assets (for example, buildings, machines, and inventories) or that have high earnings per share relative to their share price.[2]

Wouldn't it be a good idea to incorporate this into our low-risk strategy? Yes, absolutely. After all, if value investing is already a proven concept in itself, it makes perfect sense to buy cheap, low-risk stocks rather than expensive ones. But which kind of value characteristics should we focus on?

In order to answer this, let's first take another step back. Let's think about the reason why investors generally buy stocks. They buy the shares of companies to receive 'something' in return: a capital gain (if the stock price appreciates), a dividend, or both.

---

[2] The first academic study which proved that a value approach gives high returns was done by Sanjoy Basu in 1977. Many studies followed, the most prominent and most cited is Nobel Prize winner Eugene Fama's work. Some academics argue that value investing works because investors are too optimistic and overpay for growth, while other academics point to the higher risk of value stocks as an explanation for their higher returns.

Investors refer to the dividends they receive from their stock investments as 'income'.

Don't underestimate the importance of dividends. Professor Elroy Dimson estimates that about half of the total return generated by the US and UK stock markets between the years 1900 and 2000 was attributable to dividends.[3] In other words, income matters. In fact, it matters quite a lot. Dividend yield is a good yardstick for directly comparing one stock with another. The dividend should be related to the share price. For example, a stock which pays a USD 1 dividend and has a share price of USD 10 has a dividend yield of 10%. This stock is more attractive than one with a share price of USD 100 that also pays a dividend of USD 1. A 10% dividend yield is more attractive than a 1% dividend yield.

However, there is one problem in focusing on dividend yield alone. There are companies that like to pay dividends, but for other reasons – for example, dividend taxation – they may prefer to buy back shares from existing shareholders. If a company decides to buy back some of its own shares, it just means that any future profits will be shared among a smaller group of shareholders. You can also see these share buybacks as a form of 'hidden income', as, although you won't receive any cash from the company, your share of the 'profit pie' grows. If we focus only on dividend yield when selecting low-volatility stocks, we will probably miss out on those companies that buy back shares instead of distributing dividends. For this reason we prefer to focus on *both* when selecting low-volatility stocks: dividend yields and share buybacks. As both are sources of income to shareholders, I'd like to refer to this value metric as 'income'.

Income is an elegant value indicator as it favors companies that at least make profits (if they don't, it's quite a challenge to pay

---

[3] Dimson, Marsh, and Staunton (2002).

dividends or buy back stocks) while their shares are trading on the cheap. By definition, if a stock becomes expensive, the income yield will fall and other stocks will automatically become more attractive. Income also says something about management behavior, as it signals that the managers are good stewards, cautiously managing the cash and profits of a company.[4]

So that's our first additional ingredient. By focusing on low-volatility stocks which offer an appealing income, we can enhance our low-risk investment strategy even further. However, there is a potential risk if we *only* incorporate value metrics into a low-volatility strategy. We need a second ingredient. Let me explain why.

Some stocks have a low price and offer a high income yield but are 'cheap for a reason'. These stocks might look attractive, but what if the business prospects of these companies aren't so appealing? What if you find out, for example, that a low-volatility stock offers a high dividend yield, but its directors are selling subsidiaries or issuing large quantities of debt just to pay out a dividend to its shareholders? It might look like an appealing investment if you only focus on dividend yield, but in time this company could run into severe problems.

Investors like to refer to these kinds of value stocks as 'value traps'. If you fall into the trap and are won over by the appeal of an attractive valuation metric, you'll end up facing the consequences: a stock price that gradually falls into the abyss. In this situation investors often fall victim to the 'boiling frog' syndrome. According to this anecdote, a frog in a pan of water does not jump out if the water is heated gradually, and will eventually be boiled alive. Similarly, most people underreact to news when it comes in gradually and also run the risk of being 'boiled'.[5]

---

[4] Some investors refer to a firm's total payout to shareholders as a 'quality' measure. This investment style is less well defined than value investing and sometimes also includes low-risk measures in addition to profitability measures.

Let me offer you some good news right now. Momentum is the second ingredient you will need in your low-volatility portfolio. Momentum prevents you buying into such a value trap. If the price trend of a low-volatility stock with an attractive income is gradually falling, it's a bad omen. So, in order to avoid being boiled, we should enhance our low-volatility strategy by also incorporating price-trend information. By focusing on low-volatility stocks which have an appealing income and which demonstrate a positive price trend, we can steer away from these risks. Figure 8.1 shows that the hare underreacts to the worsening circumstances and ignores momentum, but the tortoise responds correctly. It notices the rising temperature, and jumps out of the pan in time to save itself.

Perhaps you've already heard the term 'price trend' in the context of how a stock price moves over a certain period of time. Analysts

FIGURE 8.1   The boiling frog metaphor refers to the human tendency to underreact to news

---

[5] Although empirically refuted, this is a powerful metaphor which explains why people tend to underreact to bad news if they receive this news gradually. See also Wikipedia: https://en.wikipedia.org/wiki/Boiling_frog.

who like to focus on price trends and patterns to judge whether a stock is a good investment or not, tend to favor stocks that follow an upward-sloping price trend. These – technical – analysts, like to say things like 'The trend is your friend'. They are convinced that stocks that have recently performed quite well (also known as winning stocks) will tend to be winners in the near future as well. They also believe that the reverse is true and that you should avoid stocks that are falling, as this trend will also continue. This phenomenon has a fancy, but commonly accepted, name too: momentum. And guess what? There is also robust academic evidence that momentum investing actually works.

A portfolio consisting of these 'winning' stocks delivers much better returns than a portfolio of 'losing' stocks. Some evidence to support momentum investing even dates back to the nineteenth century.[6] And the benefits of momentum are also evident outside equity markets, in bond, currency, and commodity markets. Investors tend to underreact to news for a period of about 12 months. Over short periods (less than one month) and long periods (longer than three years) investors tend to *overreact* to news. In most academic studies on momentum, the period observed is 12 months, without taking the last month into account. Over this one-year period, many people behave like the frog in the pan. They either fail to recognize how badly a bad firm is doing, or how well a good firm is actually doing. Momentum helps to overcome this psychological bias that plagues many of us.

Momentum not only prevents us from stepping into the value trap, or saves us from getting boiled in the pan, it also helps us to select those stocks that are on the verge of recovering to their intrinsic value at the right time. Buying low-risk stocks which offer

---

[6] The first academic study which showed this was performed by Jegadeesh and Titman in 1993. Since then, lots of additional evidence has been published, including some studies showing consistent momentum profits going back all the way to 1801. For the interested reader: Momentum in Imperial Russia, by William Goetzmann and Simon Huang, 2015 SSRN abstract number 2663482.

attractive income at a time when other investors are not willing to do so can be a wise move. But, if you want to make a profit on such an investment, you'll need the help of others. Because only when other investors understand the potential of your investment – and start buying shares – will the share price advance and momentum start to develop. So, what should you do if you like to buy stable, high-income stocks but you lack the patience required? Well, just make sure you select only those stocks with appealing momentum.

Momentum and income are a remarkably powerful combination, as they tell you how to buy the right stock at the right moment. With this insight, our quest for a way to improve our low-risk strategy comes to an end. We have now established that there are two ingredients you need to further improve an already good low-volatility strategy: you need to check if the low-risk stock's income is good and whether it is a recent 'winning' (momentum) stock. I am sure that by now you can't wait to see the results of such an improved low-volatility strategy, and so I suggest you quickly turn to the next page!

Chapter Nine

All Good Things Come in Threes

ALL GOOD THINGS COME IN THREES: you only need low-volatility, income, and momentum to build a stock portfolio that delivers high returns and low risk. But please, don't take my word for it. You should test this claim yourself by doing some rigorous fact checking. So let's get back to the spreadsheets we left behind in Chapter 3 and do some further analysis.

Just to refresh your mind a bit, in Chapter 3 we simulated what the value of two investment portfolios would have been on 1 January 2015 if we'd invested USD 100 on 1 January 1929 in either a basket of low-volatility stocks or a basket of high-volatility stocks. We created these portfolios from a universe of the largest 1,000 stocks available at each quarter throughout the period.

Each quarter we ranked these stocks according to their three-year historic volatility and bought the 100 least volatile stocks for our low-volatility portfolio and vice versa for our high-volatility portfolio. Stocks that we held in either our low- or high-volatility portfolio, but that no longer fulfilled our criteria (as their volatility was neither low nor high enough), were sold and replaced with fresh low- or high-volatility stocks. After investing in these portfolios over 86 years, the high-volatility portfolio was 'only' worth USD 21,000, while the low-volatility portfolio had a value of USD 395,000. Quite a 'satisfying' result considering we only selected stocks on the basis of their low-volatility characteristic. That's enough 'refreshment'.

But can we create the same portfolios while also taking income and momentum into account? That's easy. Remember that we want to select low-volatility stocks that also have appealing income and momentum characteristics. So we should first focus on volatility characteristics and then on income and momentum. Our starting point is the same universe as we used before: the 1,000 largest US stocks available at any point in time. We calculate the historical volatility of each stock and simply exclude the 500 stocks with the highest volatility. Just forget about this group, as we will now continue with the 500 stocks with the lowest volatility.

What unites all the stocks in this group is the common characteristic of having a relatively low amount of volatility. But not all of them have high income or positive momentum. Some have high income but terrible momentum whereas others have positive momentum and poor income. How should we deal with this?

Well, let's start ranking again. We rank the 500 low-volatility stocks on income and 12-month momentum. Each stock gets a score (1–500) based on these two factors and these scores are simply added together. Then we merge these two lists into one combined list and simply buy the first 100 stocks on this list. A top-ranked stock will have (1) low-volatility, (2) high income, and (3) good momentum. In Latin, *omne trium perfectum*, all good things come in threes, or the law of three. The tortoise graphically summarizes the formula for selecting what we term the best 'conservative' stocks.

By utilizing these combined rankings, we can make sure that a stock that has high income but terrible momentum, or the reverse,

FIGURE 9.1   The conservative stock formula

will end up somewhere in the middle of the combined list. Don't worry about getting the math on this combined ranking. It is quite simple. If a stock has a ranking of 1 on income and a ranking of 499 on momentum, it will have a combined rank of 250 and will not be considered one of the most attractive. The higher a company scores on the combination of income and momentum, the better its position on the overall ranking will be.

The last step in our portfolio construction process is straightforward and simple. All 500 low-volatility stocks in the combined list are ranked from the top score of 1 (scoring high on both income and momentum) to the bottom score of 500 (scoring poorly on both characteristics). After doing this, we just buy the top 100 stocks that have the best combined score. That's it.

Easy isn't it? First, we rank the 1,000 stocks on low-volatility characteristics, then the remaining top 500 on income and momentum. After which we simply buy the top 100 for our portfolio. The name of this portfolio? Obviously we could have given it a fancy name like 'Low-Volatility-High-Income-and-Good-Momentum Portfolio', but in line with the formula of Figure 9.1 I prefer to label this portfolio the 'conservative portfolio'. Why? Well, the formula favors those low-risk companies that 'conservatively' deploy their capital, as they would rather distribute money

to their shareholders than spend it on corporate activities themselves. The formula is also 'conservative' with regards to the timing.
These stocks are only included when their business momentum
improves and other investors have started to bid up their prices.

FIGURE 9.2   Conservative stocks versus low-volatility stocks

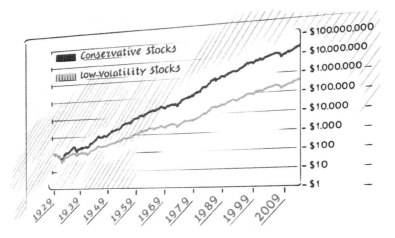

Figure 9.2 demonstrates that enhancing our low-volatility portfolio with income and momentum results in a superior portfolio. The
paradox becomes even stronger. The portfolio is characterized by very
attractive returns during the 1929–2015 period. As far back as the
Great Depression, taking the income and momentum of low-volatility stocks into account already starts to pay off and our new portfolio
of conservative stocks starts to outperform the original low-volatility
portfolio right from the outset. After the first few years, the difference between the dollar value of the conservative portfolio and the
low-volatility portfolio becomes bigger and bigger with each passing
decade. And by the time we reach 2015, the value of the conservative
portfolio is worth over USD 21 million, or 53 times the dollar value
of the low-volatility portfolio. Quite a 'satisfying' result, I would say.

So, if enhancing a low-volatility portfolio with income and
momentum to create our conservative portfolio has such strong
results, what would have been the result of investing in a portfolio

that invested in high-volatility stocks with low income and poor momentum? Well, we can investigate what would happen. I created a portfolio by first selecting the top 500 stocks in our universe with the highest volatility. As a next step I ranked these stocks first on income, then on momentum, and finally I calculated the combined score. I then proceeded to create a 'bad' portfolio that invested in the 100 stocks that ranked lowest on this list. In a nutshell, this portfolio invested in high-volatility stocks that were expensive and had poor momentum. How should we label this portfolio?

FIGURE 9.3   A risky portfolio does not make you rich

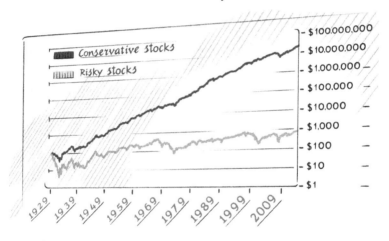

Looking at the graph in Figure 9.3 I think 'risky portfolio' is an appropriate name for it. Risky, as the value of the USD 100 that you invest on 1 January 1929 quickly evaporates to less than USD 10 during the Great Depression. It then takes 15 years to recover your losses (although only temporarily) and start generating positive returns. Unfortunately, the joy is short-lived, because 45 (!) years after you started your portfolio, its value drops below USD 100 again. Admittedly, after 86 years it has made some 'profits', as the final value on New Year's Day 2015 is slightly over USD 750. The fact that I say 'profits' doesn't mean I'm being cynical, but is related to the definition of the word. Although you made a profit of over USD 650, if you measure this in real US dollars, corrected for inflation, a different picture emerges.

Inflation destroys the purchasing power of your money. In other words, USD 100 buys you fewer goods in 2015 than it did in 1929. In fact, USD 100 in 1929 had the same purchasing power as USD 1,373 in 2015.[1] So the increase from USD 100 to USD 750 does not even make up for inflation. You would need USD 1,373 to break even, so the USD 750 in 2015 results in a 45% loss in purchasing power compared to 1929. That's what I call a real loss.

Combined low-volatility, income, and momentum are three mighty ingredients that can make a huge difference to your overall wealth. And you don't need to wait 86 years to reap the rewards of this powerful trio.

Take a look at Figure 9.3 again. After just two decades, there is a huge difference in what you would have earned from the conservative portfolio compared to the risky portfolio. On New Year's Day 1949, you would already have had a 'ten bagger'[2] by investing in the conservative portfolio, while you would still be facing losses if you'd invested in the risky portfolio. Investing in conservative stocks is a long-term winning strategy. The average compounded return is 15% per annum over the full period.

Figure 9.4 shows the returns per decade, both for the conservative portfolio and the risky portfolio. In every decade the conservative portfolio beats the risky portfolio. That is nine wins out of nine, achieved with lower risk. The investment paradox is persistent through time. Whether it was during the Great Depression, the go-go years of the 1960s, or during the magnificent 1990s

---

[1] See www.dollartimes.com/inflation/inflation.php?amount=100&year=1929 to calculate the loss in purchasing power over time.

[2] Jargon for an investment that appreciates to ten times its initial purchase price. The term 'ten bagger' was coined by legendary fund manager Peter Lynch in his book *One Up On Wall Street*. Lynch coined the term because he is an avid baseball fan, and 'bag' is a colloquial term for base; thus, 'ten bagger' represents two home runs and a double, or the stock equivalent of a hugely successful baseball play.

FIGURE 9.4   Conservative stocks: never a lost decade

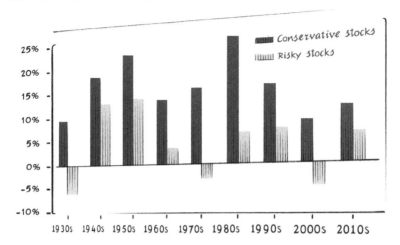

when the stock market boomed, the returns were higher and more stable, varying around 15%. Sometimes they rose above 20% in the 1980s, and dipped slightly below 10% in the 2000s, a period characterized by two major stock market corrections (2001 and 2008). As expected, the risky portfolio shows much weaker returns, averaging around 3% over the whole period. The returns are especially low during more difficult decades such as the 1930s and the 2000s.

The return difference is a staggering 12% per year. This is not only a big difference, but it is also very robust or 'significant' as academics would say.[3] Significant means that the chance that this return difference is just the outcome of sheer luck is very limited. In this case, the probability is 1 in a *quintillion* (10^{18}) instances.

Let's take another look at statistics. Please take a look at Figure 9.5. What is the chance of dying as the result of a shark attack? In 2014, three people out of a world population of 7 billion died in a shark attack. This gives a probability of 1 in 2.3 billion that you will die due

---

[3] To directly compare the return difference of both portfolios on a like-for-like basis, you scale up the conservative portfolio and scale down the risky portfolio, also correcting for financing costs. The resulting *t*-value is 9.4, far above the critical 2.0 level. To put this result into a practical perspective, such an enormous *t*-value corresponds with a probability of 1 in a *quintillion* instances.

FIGURE 9.5   A deadly shark attack tomorrow is more likely than a rejection of the paradox

to a shark attack in any given year, or an even smaller probability of 1 in 850 billion on any given day. Although it is extremely low, the probability of facing such a tragedy is still 1 million times higher than the probability that the return difference between our conservative portfolio and the risky portfolio is due to sheer luck. In fact, given the level of significance of our results, the probability that you will be bitten to death by a shark tomorrow is, in fact, higher than the probability that the extra return the conservative portfolio offered is just the outcome of sheer luck. Who said statistics aren't fun? [4]

And finally, what if we compare the conservative portfolio with the stock market average? We know we shouldn't compare too

---

[4] Let me place this robust result in the context of a recent and still ongoing debate among academics. The leading science journals have become more aware and critical of so-called 'false positives'; results that *seem* to be significant but, in fact, aren't. As many researchers are encouraged to publish significant results, they have a clear incentive to go 'data fishing': undertaking actions just to get a seemingly robust *t*-value. This understandable human behavior is seriously threatening the quality of science, as many studies cannot be replicated. The most obvious solution to this problem is simply to raise the bar. Campbell Harvey, a former *Journal of Finance* editor, suggests increasing the critical *t*-value for evaluating investment strategies from 2 to 4.

much, but let's do it. On average, the conservative portfolio beats this 'benchmark', generating higher returns at a lower level of risk. The difference in annual returns is 4%. The power of compounding makes this difference in returns amount to a portfolio value of USD 21 million for the conservative portfolio versus USD 870,000 for the average stock portfolio. You see, all good things really come in threes!

So, these conservative stocks beat the risky stocks and even beat the market average. But what kind of stocks are we talking about? To get a better feeling and understanding of the investment paradox, I'll take you on a safari as we go in search of tortoises and hares on the stock market.

Chapter Ten

Spotting Tortoises and Hares

So, WHAT DO THESE ATTRACTIVE CONSERVATIVE stocks look like? What kind of business are they doing? In what kind of industry are they operating? And can you detect a wealth-killing risky stock, which should not end up in your portfolio? In this chapter we're going to shed some light on the tortoises and the hares of the stock market.

But before doing so, I would like to tell you more about a commonly used risk metric in addition to volatility: beta. Beta is a widely used risk metric and it measures the risk of a stock and how much it contributes to the risk of the market. Beta is similar to volatility, but can be understood in a more simple way. A stock with a beta below 1 has low risk, while a stock with a beta above 1 has high risk. If a stock has a beta of 1.5, it should go up 15% when the market goes up 10%. And a stock with a beta of 0.5 will go up 5% if the market goes up 10%. So, a risky stock has a beta above 1, easy to remember, isn't it?

Beta is easier to use than volatility as a risk measure as it can be understood in a straightforward way. A volatility of 25% can be a high number or a low number, as it depends on the volatility of other stocks in the market. For example, during a period of panic and crisis on the stock market, the volatility of all stocks can become pretty high. At such times, a stock with 25% volatility can be classified as low risk, while in a less stressful season on the stock market – let's say a bull market – the overall level of stock volatility can be relatively low and a stock with 25% volatility may then be classified as high risk. In other words, volatility is time-varying, just like the weather. For beta, the interpretation is simpler and more stable over time. A low-risk stock simply has a beta below 1. That's it. Most financial newspapers or investing websites give the betas of stocks. But don't worry: the stock-market paradox holds regardless of whether you use beta or volatility.[1]

Now let's take a look at several well-known large international stocks shown in Table 10.1. This table shows some common stock characteristics for the five largest US, German, Japanese, and Chinese (Hong Kong) companies, so 20 in total.

For each stock we show the beta, which varies around 1. The table also shows the dividend yield and the 52-week price change. As explained in Chapter 8, the dividend yield is the amount of dividend a company pays out to its shareholders, measured as a percentage of the stock price.[2] In contrast to beta, a high value is better than a low value for this indicator. The 52-week price change is very straightforward, as it simply measures the stock trend. When we compare this trend with the trends of other stocks, it is called momentum. We use a one-year look-back period

---

[1] The investment paradox also exists when stocks are sorted based on beta, although the results are slightly stronger when stocks are sorted on volatility. One open research question is why this is the case.

[2] Dividend yield is usually the largest part of the income paid to shareholders. Since most data providers report dividend yield, we use this as our best proxy for income.

TABLE 10.1   20 largest US, German, Japanese, and Chinese stocks – June 2016

Country – Company name	Beta	Dividend yield (%)	52-week price change (%)
United States			
Apple	0.9	1.7	27
Alphabet	0.9	0.0	35
Microsoft	1.0	2.7	10
Berkshire Hathaway	0.8	0.0	−1
Exxon Mobil	0.9	3.3	6
Germany			
SAP	0.8	1.6	8
Siemens	0.9	3.6	3
Bayer	1.0	2.9	−33
Deutsche Telekom	0.7	3.4	2
Daimler	1.5	5.3	−28
Japan			
Toyota	1.1	3.7	−34
NTT DoCoMo	0.6	2.6	23
Japan Tobacco	0.9	2.6	−3
KDDI	0.8	2.0	14
Mitsubishi UFJ	1.6	3.4	−42
Hong Kong			
China Mobile	0.5	3.3	−14
ICBC	1.4	6.8	−39
Tencent Holdings	1.1	0.3	9
PetroChina	1.0	2.0	−42
China Construction Bank	1.2	6.6	−36

because it is commonly used in most studies on momentum and because the signal is more stable than for shorter look-back periods (e.g. six months), resulting in less turnover. Still, this measure is most volatile and can often completely change after one year. This means these specific 52-week price changes are just a snapshot in time, used mainly for illustration purposes, certainly not to give any kind of investment recommendation.

What can we say about the 20 big shots? A lot. Let's focus first on a big US stock: Apple. This company has a beta below 1, pays out some dividend, and has positive momentum. So, pretty stable at this point in time. And what is the best low-risk stock on this list? In order to get the answer, just check the betas of each single stock and remember: below 1 is good. Berkshire Hathaway has a beta below 1. Outside the US, China Mobile is doing a good job with a beta of 0.5. But is it a conservative stock? Maybe, but not at this moment in time. The company's dividend yield is OK at 3.3%, but the momentum. . . Well, it isn't *that* bad, but it isn't positive either.

Let's turn things around now. Can you spot the most risky stock on this list? That's an easy one. Mitsubishi and Daimler clearly have high betas of 1.6 and 1.5, respectively. These risky companies pay nice dividends, but the momentum is clearly negative. Because of this risk and the bad momentum, these stocks do not satisfy the three criteria. They could be labeled hares at this point in time. If you had bought these stocks in the past, you might have sold them by now, as two of the three ingredients are giving a negative signal. Two large Japanese stocks look attractive: both NTT and KDDI score well on all three measures at this point in time.

So what's next? Should we focus only on these 20 large companies and just pick the best based on their beta, dividend yield, and momentum? No, I have a far better idea. Instead of focusing only on the largest, let's consider *all* the listed companies in these markets.

The benefit of this is three-fold. First, the probability that we'll find some attractive companies in each country is higher if we include thousands of stocks rather than only 20 large caps. Second, you can do the screening using the most recent stock information available. Third, you will have enough flexibility to spot the tortoises and the hares in any market or sector you like.

Don't worry if you don't live in any of these four places. I'll show you how to build a conservative stock portfolio even if you live in another country like Brazil, South Korea, or the Netherlands. So, now that we have learned what tortoises look like, it's time to figure out how exactly we can catch them!

.

Chapter Eleven

Slice and Dice, But Do It Wisely

HOW DO WE CATCH THOSE STEADY TORTOISES? How do we find the right conservative stocks to put into our portfolio? Should we calculate each stock's risk, income, and momentum before ranking them like we've done in Chapter 9? Ideally yes, but that would require 'some' work. A slightly less sophisticated and less time-consuming approach is available in the form of stock screeners.

Stock screeners are tools that investors can use to select those stocks that meet their requirements. They contain the latest market data and are easy to use. You just have to indicate which stock characteristics you are interested in and to which market you want to apply them. You could screen for US-listed stocks that have a dividend yield above 4%, for example. A stock screener will provide you with a list of companies that meet this criterion. These stock screeners are widely available. And although some come in the form of standalone software, most are available online.[1]

Most of these screeners do a pretty good job when it comes down to filtering a universe to find stocks with good income or momentum. An abundance of metrics, variables, or characteristics is available for the income or momentum investor. However, for the low-risk investor, who is looking for beta or volatility measures, the toolkit is mostly quite limited. Only some screeners enable you to screen on beta. The fact that stock screeners don't devote much attention to stocks' risk characteristics might be another reason why low-risk investing works. Apparently, most investors don't focus on a stock's riskiness and most stock screeners don't help them either.

But, going back to our screener, let's put some tools to work and start the engines of a decent stock screener: Google Stock Screener.[2] I have chosen to use this screener for several reasons. First of all, it's simple to use. On its website, you just select the few filters that you need, set the right thresholds (minimum or maximum criteria), and this screener automatically shows you the companies. Second, it's an international stock screener. Whereas other screeners focus only on a US equity universe, Google Stock Screener can be applied to any stock market. So, a brief note to all Japanese investors: *Anata wa, Nihon no zyouzyou meigarachuu mottomo anteishiteiru meigaragun o sentaku surutameni, Nihon no yunibāsu o sentaku suru koto mo dekimasu!*[3] Third, Google has extensive data coverage. For example, it includes beta as a characteristic and it covers a lot of individual stock listings. And last – and not unimportant for a savvy investor like me – it's available at no

---

[1] If you have an online brokerage account, you can use your broker's stock screener. In addition, the website www.paradoxinvesting.com gives an overview of different online stock screeners.

[2] See: www.google.com/finance#stockscreener.

[3] Translation: you can select a Japanese universe in order to filter for the best conservative stocks that are listed in Japan!

charge. Ready? Well, let's start slicing and dicing (and I'll show you how to do it wisely too. . .).

FIGURE 11.1   Google Stock Screener – Copyright: Google

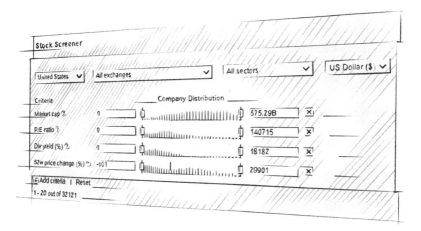

As the snapshot of the screener in Figure 11.1 shows, the online tool looks pretty simple to use. In the upper part of the figure, you'll notice that the initial start-up screener is applied to stocks from all possible sectors that are listed on any of the US exchanges. If you wish to narrow down the screening to a particular country, exchange, or sector, you can do so by selecting the drop-down boxes. For now, let's stick to the standard universe settings that are shown.

Google lists four default criteria: market cap, price/earnings (P/E) ratio, dividend yield, and the price change over the last 52 weeks. If you want to know how each criterion is measured, just do a mouse-over on the question mark behind each one to get your answer. No filter has been applied to the screener's start-up screen, so the minimum and maximum for each criterion are automatically set at the lower and upper bounds. As a result, the screener lists over 32,000 stocks, or the entire US stock market. Besides these four criteria, you should add beta as your risk criterion, under stock metrics and 'last price' as an additional criterion so you can filter out penny stocks.

Now that we have chosen the right metrics to screen for conservative stocks, it's time to adjust the settings. Let's first deal with all the penny stocks and stocks with above-average beta. If we put in a minimal price of USD 1 and a maximal beta of 1.0 in the right fields, the number of stocks will drop significantly from about 32,000 to 13,000. This is a bit of a reduction, but it's still a very long list. So it also makes sense to put in a minimal market capitalization filter to exclude stocks with a small market capitalization, the so-called micro-caps. We can do this by setting the filter for market capitalization at USD 1 billion. As a result, the number of stocks drops further to about 5,000.[4] You see, with just a few clicks and some key strokes we are moving towards a more manageable number, but we are not there yet.

The two other ingredients are income and momentum. First, we cannot filter for buybacks, so we set the minimal dividend yield at 3%. Companies with this minimal yield are either cheaply priced or distribute a relatively large part of their profits to shareholders. And it is wise to limit the maximal P/E ratio to 30, which can be translated into an earnings yield of 3%. Second, we filter for momentum. But which criterion should we use for momentum? During our simulations we didn't apply a strict absolute filter for momentum. We ranked each stock on its one-year price change and sorted them from high to low. In order to make your life easy, just require each of the stocks to at least have a positive 52-week price change.[5] In other words, just set the minimal passing percentage for momentum to 0%.

---

[4] Having a minimal market capitalization filter in place is important for professional investors like mutual fund managers. Most of these investors need to make sure they select stocks that are easily tradeable, like liquid large cap stocks. Assuming that your portfolio is somewhat smaller in size, you can easily reduce the level for this criterion.

[5] Be aware that the number of stocks a screener will find for you also depends on market conditions. For example, if the stock market plummets and most stocks decline by 50%, you'll probably find fewer companies that exceed the USD 1 billion threshold. The same principle applies to 52-week price change.

As a result, the number of stocks to choose from shrinks even further from about 5,000 to around 100. These remaining stocks have what it takes to classify as low-risk stock with good upside potential. The types of company that the screener finds will make an interesting list and will vary over time. In general, defensive companies in defensive sectors will appear, for example, telecom and utility stocks. But some technology companies will satisfy these criteria too. Slicing and dicing is also an effective way of dealing with your own emotions. A screener doesn't have any prejudices with regards to particular stocks, which you might have. So just let the output surprise you. Since companies that show up in the screener are not always the same, I recommend you to run the analysis yourself in order to find out.

A fun feature of the Google Stock Screener is that you can apply it to other markets as well. It is also practical as it gives you the opportunity to diversify your portfolio using conservative stocks from different countries.[6] For example, if you want to find Japanese conservative stocks, you can just select 'Japan' in the drop-down menu at the top of the stock screener. You will probably have to adjust the settings of some criteria in order to make them fit your foreign market of choice. If the screener gives you a smaller number of conservative stocks to choose from, you can adjust the criteria. If you want to have a longer list, it's probably better to be less strict on criteria such as market capitalization, dividend yield, or momentum. I wouldn't recommend relaxing the maximal threshold for beta, since reducing risk is the most important element. Just remember that we want to find *conservative* stocks: low-risk stocks that also offer attractive income and good momentum.

---

[6] The paradox is very robust and can be found in all international stock markets. In 2007, David Blitz and I showed that low-risk stocks beat high-risk stocks not only in the US, but also in Europe and Japan. A few years later, in 2011, we documented similar results for 19 emerging stock markets. See also Chapter 16 of this book (The Paradox Is Everywhere).

It is wise to extend your hunt for a larger group of tortoises to different countries, as if you invest in only a few stocks in your home market you will end up with an under-diversified portfolio. Having a diversified portfolio is really something that you should pay attention to. I stress these words as it is a well-known phenomenon (and problem) that investors often don't diversify enough. Most investors hold concentrated portfolios consisting of only a few stocks, mostly from their home country. This leads to investment portfolios which carry too much *unnecessary* risk. As diversification is the only free lunch available to investors, it's probably best to secure your seat at the table by investing in more than just a handful of stocks. I would recommend creating a portfolio that consists of at least 50 individual stocks from different sectors and different countries. And if you can create an even bigger portfolio of up to 150 names, that's even better. Because when it comes to building conservative stock portfolios, 10 stocks are too few, while 1,000 are too many. So please be wise and diversify when you start slicing and dicing.

Still, I do understand that it's difficult for an individual investor to invest in so many individual stocks listed on so many different foreign exchanges. Let alone keep up to speed on – probably on a weekly basis – corporate actions like mergers, dividend distributions, stock-splits, acquisitions, and so on. The portfolio will also need to be rebalanced on a regular basis because stock characteristics change over time. Frequent rebalancing keeps your portfolio in shape, as it stays invested in the best conservative stocks. But the more you rebalance, the more commission you have to pay to your broker. To balance these opposing forces, it's best to rebalance your portfolio on a quarterly or semi-annual basis. When you do rebalance, remember to make the sell criteria much lower than the buy criteria in order to also save on transaction costs.

So there you have it! Using a good stock screener enables you to easily select conservative stocks in the stock market of your choice. The hardest part is perhaps managing the portfolio itself. In order to build a well-diversified portfolio, you should invest in quite a lot of different conservative stocks. Diversifying across sectors is easier than across countries. Also, you cannot just 'sit back and relax' because you will need to rebalance the portfolio along the way while keeping trading costs at bay. If you are an avid individual stock investor yourself and you like to deal with such a challenge, this could be the road to Rome that really suits you. But if you're not, it is probably wise to let a professional manage your portfolio. So, let's now explore the 'sit-back-and-relax' option!

Chapter Twelve

Sit Back and Relax

MANAGING A CONSERVATIVE STOCK PORTFOLIO yourself can be a daunting challenge as you need to make numerous decisions along the way. However, if you choose to let somebody else do it for you, you only need to make one: which investment vehicle are you going to put your money in? Although it's only one decision, I'm sure you'll agree with me that it's an important one. But please don't worry, the difference between all the available alternatives is just the difference between 'good' and 'better', as there are no really bad low-risk stock portfolios available. Nevertheless, in this chapter I will explain how you can make the right decision.

If you decide to let somebody else run your investment portfolio, you basically have two options: you either select a fund manager who tracks an index or you select one who pursues an active strategy.[1] Both approaches have their own advantages.

---

[1] To be honest, the sentence '*You basically have two options* sounds like a waitress in a restaurant in a communist country who's explaining all the available menu options to me. In reality, the world of passive and active investing is not just black and white, there are also many shades of gray.

In general, index investing means that your investments will be managed according to the composition of a certain index, like the S&P 500 or the German DAX 30. An index fund or tracker aims to mirror the performance characteristics of the index by simply replicating it. In order to ensure their investments track the performance of a particular index, most managers create a portfolio that contains the same stocks and weightings as that index. The costs associated with an index tracker tend to be lower than the costs of active funds and transparency is higher. In fact, they are fully transparent.

But this transparency can also be a disadvantage. Too much transparency is not good. If everybody knows that a tracker is going to buy a certain kind of stock in a sizable quantity, chances are that opportunistic investors will get in ahead of the trade and front-run the orders. In fact, these investment vehicles provide so much transparency that everyone in the market can figure out which trades will be executed. This could result in losses for those investors who track publicly available indices, especially if these indices are popular and their constituents change significantly each year.

This weakness of transparent indices could be a valid reason to choose an active and less transparent strategy. Changes in your portfolio will be safeguarded from 'predatory' traders. On the other hand, if you buy into a tracker, you tend to pay a lower fee.

So, if you would like to hand over the management of your low-risk portfolio to an investment manager, you have these two options available: tracking a public index or investing in a proprietary active strategy. Let's first explore the possibilities of low-risk index trackers.

Low-risk indices give you exposure to a broad basket of around 100 to 300 low-risk stocks. These indices are usually tracked by Exchange Traded Funds (ETFs) and sometimes by passive mutual funds, also known as index funds. As these ETFs are listed on an exchange, you can trade easily and whenever you want and gain exposure to a low-risk index without having to invest a large sum. They also save you the hassle of managing over 100 stocks yourself. Given their modest fees, they appear to be a good option for an investor who is looking for a transparently managed low-volatility strategy. And on top of this, they are easy to find.

Just as you can apply a stock screener to find low-risk stocks, you can apply ETF screeners to select the right low-risk ETF. Most online brokers provide these tools to help you find your way in the ETF jungle. There are also numerous websites where you can screen a universe for low-risk ETFs.[2]

ETF Database (ETFdb) has an ETF screener that anyone can access and which is easy to use.[3] Its website lists over 1,200 different equity ETFs which can be further filtered using size, investment strategy, region, sector, or investment style parameters. In order to slice and dice all US-listed low-volatility ETFs, you just have to enter 'low volatility' in the last input box (investment style) of the ETFdb website.

By doing so, the screener will highlight more than 40 different investment vehicles available to investors who are looking for a low-volatility ETF. This number has gone up over the years, offering clients more choice. All matching ETFs are shown in an overview at the bottom of the ETFdb webpage. Figure 12.1 provides a snapshot of this ETF screener.

This screener ranks all available ETFs according to size (assets in million USD). Most of these ETFs mimic two low-risk indices: the MSCI Minimum Volatility Index and the S&P Low Volatility Index. These minimal volatility and low volatility indices are available for different markets: from 'USA only' to European stocks, from global to emerging markets, and from mid- and small-cap to S&P 500 stocks.

---

[2] For an overview of ETF screeners, see www.paradoxinvesting.com which lists an overview of different ETF screening websites.

[3] See: www.ETFdb.com/screener.

FIGURE 12.1   Selecting low-risk ETFs at www.ETFdb.com/screener – Copyright: ETFdb.com

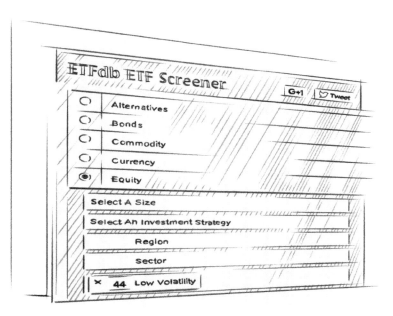

So, which of these ETFs should we focus on? Well, given the fact that we're aiming to find a vehicle that gives us exposure to low-risk stocks, why don't we investigate the two most popular trackers? These multi-billion funds track two different low-risk indices. Their ticker codes are SPLV and USMV.

First, the S&P 500 low-volatility portfolio (SPLV) tracks a low-volatility index. It measures the one-year volatility of all stocks in the S&P 500 Index and ranks them from low to high. Then it simply buys the 100 stocks with the lowest volatility. Each quarter the index is rebalanced and those stocks that no longer fall into the group with the lowest volatility within the S&P 500 will be replaced. The average holding period for a stock is two years. Simple, isn't it? This ETF really offers a pretty straightforward and simple way of creating a low-volatility portfolio. But perhaps you'd prefer more complexity?

Second, the iShares Edge MSCI Min Vol USA ETF (USMV) tracks a different index which is also in the name of the fund. The methodology that forms the basis for the construction of this index is more complex than the simple ranking approach of the SPLV. The starting point for this index is the MSCI USA Index. It consists of 600 large and mid-cap stocks. A statistical optimizer uses an algorithm to construct a low-volatility portfolio from these 600 stocks. The stocks are not only selected on the basis of their standalone volatility, but also on their contribution to total portfolio volatility. The index is rebalanced twice a year and the average holding period for a stock is five years. The number of stocks is around 170. Since it is quite challenging to pinpoint exactly how and why this statistical optimizer constructs this index, some label this methodology, as illustrated in Figure 12.2, a 'black box'.

In general, the SPLV, with its ranking approach, is elegant and straightforward. The USMV is more complex, but this index is better diversified across sectors and companies. However, neither takes income or momentum into account. As you may recall from Chapter 9, it is abiding by the 'rule of three' (looking at risk, but also including income and momentum characteristics) that can lead to significant wealth creation. The annual return difference was 3%. The flip side is that there are also low-volatility stocks

FIGURE 12.2   A statistical optimizer uses complex algorithms

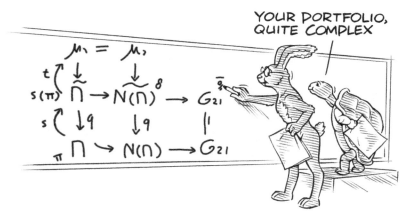

which can also perform 3% worse if they have low income and weak momentum characteristics. So please do not forget the rule of three when buying a low-volatility index tracker.

The alternative to an index is a proprietary active strategy. Active low-volatility managers have the freedom and full discretion to select what are, in their view, the best low-risk stocks which also offer good upside potential. Most of them use academically inspired stock-selection models, which often include income-related factors and sometimes also momentum factors. They tend to give some explanation of their strategy on their websites or newsletters, but not full transparency.

In order to find a good active low-volatility manager, you could also ask your investment advisor or a specialized investment consultant like Morningstar for some help. Most of these investment advisors pay close attention to the manager's investment philosophy and investment process as well as to the quality of the investment team and the performance of their low-volatility strategies.

And here comes the disclosure: of course I'm a bit biased as a portfolio manager of a family of low-risk funds, so let me be completely open here. Robeco started offering 'Conservative Equity' funds in 2006. The process used is similar to the one discussed in this book, but it deviates from it – especially in the implementation phase – on several points. I can quite understand your desire to smile when I tell you this low-risk strategy is better than the other active funds and trackers... Trust me, but don't just blindly believe what I say, try instead to be skeptical and make up your own mind.

Let's take a look at some of the active low-risk equity funds available in the market. I have listed seven large, low-volatility funds of experienced fund managers in the overview in Table 12.1. These investment teams have at least 10 years' experience and all run multi-billion US dollar strategies. The fund names vary but usually refer to the lower risk.

TABLE 12.1   Seven large and experienced low-risk equity managers[4]

Fund name	Asset manager	Location team
Conservative Equities	Robeco	Rotterdam, The Netherlands
Low Volatility	Analytic Investors	Los Angeles, United States
Managed Volatility	Acadian	Boston, United States
Minimum Variance	Unigestion	Geneva, Switzerland
MinRisk Equities	Quoniam	Frankfurt, Germany
Stable Equities	Nordea	Copenhagen, Denmark
Structured Equity	Invesco	Frankfurt, Germany

As you can see, low-risk investing seems to be a 'European thing', as five out of seven managers have European roots. Although not shown in Table 12.1, a Nordic, Dutch, and Swiss low-volatility manager occupy the top three positions in terms of assets under management.[5]

Morningstar is useful when searching for ETFs, but also for searching for and comparing different actively managed funds. It has a global presence and offers its services in many languages tailored to country specifics. Its website shows details of mutual funds, and for registered users it also provides detailed fund reports. I usually use the Dutch website where you can easily find all the available strategies available to private investors. Although they cover a lot of funds (around 30,000 funds are listed on its Dutch website), finding the low-volatility funds of the asset managers mentioned in Table 12.1 is quite easy. Just enter the fund name in the search box at the top of Morningstar's website and it will locate the right fund.

To illustrate, I have analyzed the two most popular trackers and two popular active funds for emerging markets. All four strategies shown in Table 12.2 have more than USD 1 billion in assets

[4] For more figures, see: www.paradoxinvesting.com.
[5] Interestingly, these three countries have the highest score on the Human Development Index too. Do they foster a culture of prudence or is this just a coincidence? Nah, I'm probably too quick to jump to conclusions.

TABLE 12.2   Four emerging market low-volatility strategies

Name	Strategy	Start date
iShares Edge MSCI Emerging Markets Minimum Volatility	Tracker	October 2011
Powershares S&P Emerging Markets Low Volatility	Tracker	January 2012
Robeco Emerging Conservative Equities	Active fund	February 2011
Unigestion-Global Equities Emerging Markets	Active fund	March 2010

under management, so they represent a large client base. They were all launched in the period between May 2010 and January 2012. One thing they all have in common is their risk characteristics. Morningstar helps us out by showing the three-year volatility and three-year beta of these funds, which tend to be in line with each other. They all have significantly lower beta and volatility than the market. The management fees for the active funds are higher than those for the index trackers, which is also an important aspect to consider. Still, the performance is indicated net of fees, so that helps you to make a fair comparison. The dividend yields of the active funds are higher than the trackers. From a valuation perspective, as measured by the P/E ratio, the fund managers of active funds seem to be doing a better job in selecting the right stocks.

Now it's time for a brief pause, as I need to confess something to you. . .

Yes, I do have something to confess. Perhaps I was a bit too easy going when I said that you can just 'sit back and relax' and let somebody else manage your low-volatility or conservative stock portfolio. Because you cannot just completely walk away from such a portfolio once you've selected a passive tracker or hired a more active portfolio manager. Most of these managers will do a great job for you, but every once in a while you'll have to check just how able they are when it comes to delivering low-volatility or conservative stock returns over time. Another handy tip is to program your search engine to send you an alert when your fund is in the news.[6] This will help you better monitor your fund in a relaxed way.

And what's more, it's not only about selecting the right manager, one who's able to distinguish between a good and a bad low-risk stock, you also need to try to figure out whether that fund manager is patient enough. Keen to know what I am getting at? I bet you are. So, as you are obviously still reading this book, you might as well turn another page so that we can focus on that good old virtue of patience.

---

[6] For example, Google Alerts (www.google.com/alerts) or Talkwalker (www.talkwalker.com/en/alerts).

Trade Little, Be Patient

WHETHER YOU BUILD A LOW-RISK STOCK PORTFOLIO yourself, or put your money to work in a low-risk fund, at least some trading is needed to get exposure to the right stocks. However, for investors like you and me, trading in itself is a loser's game as there are transaction costs involved. From this perspective it would be great if we didn't have to trade at all.

Just think about it: even if we didn't have to pay any transaction costs or management fees, active investing would still be zero sum game. Your gain is someone else's loss and the other way around. John Bogle, a US investor and entrepreneur, is famous for explaining this truth to a large audience of investors and urging them to just stop trading and passively buy and hold the total market. Doing so not only saves transaction costs, but also brings down other costs involved with active management. Bogle is right, as, on average, transaction costs are long-term wealth 'eaters'. Being patient pays off. His advice is being followed by a growing number of investors, as passive investing is on the rise. The company he founded is one of the largest asset managers in the world today.

Despite this increase in passive investing, we still trade stocks too much. *Way* too much. What's more, every decade we seem to trade more than the previous decade. The level of annual stock turnover has been above 100% since the 1990s, after decades of low turnover from the 1940s to the 1970s. Current turnover levels imply that, on average, investors hold on to a stock for less than one year. The graph in Figure 13.1 is from an academic article by Kenneth French published in 2008. It shows the rise in annual turnover for US stocks. As you can see, the high levels of trading in the Roaring Twenties came to an end with the crash of 1929. The Great Depression of the 1930s marked a change in trading behavior which lasted for decades. The virtuous 'low-trading culture' of the 1950s disappeared at the start of the bull market in the 1980s.

But why is this a problem? Isn't trading cheap nowadays? Yes, it is. The rise of electronic trading has made the cost of a single transaction much lower. Most trading is not expensive anymore. However, the formula 'transactions = costs' still holds true in the twenty-first century as much as it did throughout the twentieth century. And

FIGURE 13.1   Annual turnover US stocks in percent, 1926–2007

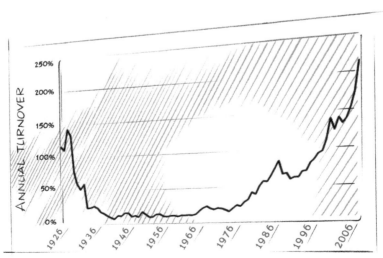

all this excessive trading is expensive for us and society. Only brokers profit from our collective behavior. The money wasted on excessive trading could also have been used for more useful purposes such as poverty reduction, healthcare, education, or buying a nice car.

But I don't want to give you the wrong idea. Of course we do need *some* trading as it helps ensure our portfolios are always exposed to, for example, the best low-risk stocks. For society too, a decent amount of trading is necessary to ensure that markets function properly. But just like many other things in life, you can have too much of a good thing and excessive trading should be avoided. You could say that the golden mean also applies to patience and trading. If you have too much patience, you stop trading completely and become fully passive. If you have too little patience, you probably trade excessively.

But why, oh why, do we all trade so much? Aren't we just trading so much because it has become so inexpensive to do so? Well, obviously lower costs as a result of cheap electronic trading play a role. However, during the 1920s, at a time when transaction costs were much higher, turnover levels were also above 100%. So trading costs don't seem to be the only determinant of our trading behavior.

According to academic literature, excessive trading might be related to overconfidence. You can be classified as being an overconfident person if you believe you are really better than average, while, in fact, you are below average. By definition, we cannot *all* be above average. Some will be, but others won't. In one famous study, 93% of US drivers thought that they were above average.[1]

Terrance Odean, a US finance professor, analyzed the broker account data of 10,000 investors and found that excessive trading

---

[1] See Ola Svenson's study (February 1981). 'Are We All Less Risky and More Skillful Than Our Fellow Drivers?'

takes place in these broker accounts. He relates the amount of trading to overconfidence and gender. Interestingly, he shows that female investors do better than male investors. Indeed, women seem to do a better job than men.[2]

Do you know why? Well, it's not that women are better traders. Before any trading costs are taken into account, they perform in line with men. In other words, if trading costs didn't exist, both sexes would show equal results. It is simply due to the fact that women trade less than men, which leads to lower trading costs and higher after-cost returns. It shouldn't come as a surprise that this phenomenon on gender has also been picked up outside academia, as we all seem to love these kinds of male/female studies.

Overconfidence can be linked to a hormone called testosterone. Let's look at this on a more personal level. In 2015 I carried out some bio-finance research and tested the relationship between testosterone and overconfidence in 52 male investment professionals. It was quite a funny thing to do, because we took several saliva samples. Just pause here for a moment and try to imagine the scene. Over 50 men in suits spitting into small plastic tubes, which were directly frozen and sent for analysis to a laboratory somewhere in Germany. The outcome? Well, almost all the men with higher levels of testosterone were overconfident while those with lower levels suffered less from this bias. Given this information, you might want to watch out if your fund manager of choice seems to have too many Popeye-like traits!

Besides these hormonal effects, excessive trading could also be caused by the incentive structures in professional portfolio management. Perhaps fund managers trade too much because

---

[2] See Brad Barber's and Terrance Odean's study (2001): 'Boys Will Be Boys: Gender, Overconfidence, and Common Stock Investment'.

their clients cannot distinguish between 'actively' doing nothing and 'simply' doing nothing. Even if they manage to control their hormones, portfolio managers can still trade excessively just to show their clients and bosses that they are doing something to earn their high management fees.

The increase in the amount of assets managed by professionals only magnifies this problem. This, combined with lower transaction costs, might explain the increase in trading activity that has occurred over the past few decades. People might consider overconfidence as irrational behavior, as it leads to lower net returns. In fact, it is a negative feedback mechanism because the results of your deeds are visible if you trade too much. But from the perspective of a portfolio manager, over-trading might indicate good investment skills, even if it leads to a worse result for the client.

Given all these insights, should we just follow Bogle's advice and stop trading altogether? Well, given the evidence that excessive trading hurts returns and is caused either by human biases or by the structure of the mutual fund industry, you might justifiably be tempted to conclude that it would be better to stop trading altogether. After all, one of the main advantages of a buy-and-hold investment strategy is that trading costs are brought back to almost zero. Both implementation costs and management fees are lower too, while liquidity and transparency are very high. These factors probably explain the steady rise of passive market-capitalization-weighted investing: lower fees, lower transaction costs, and maximal transparency.

However, passive buy-and-hold market investing also assumes the stock market to be fully efficient. With the risk of confusing you with another paradox, if everyone were to attempt to invest passively, the market would become highly inefficient, as no prices would be set anymore. Trading needs to take place so investors know what the value of any single share is. Trading is necessary to ensure fair prices and the efficient allocation of capital in a market economy.

So, if an investor buys a market-index tracker, he also assumes the market is fully efficient, which is not the case. High-risk stocks give low returns and these stocks should not be in your portfolio. In fact, they are bad for your wealth. Therefore, *some* trading is required to stay invested in the right stocks – whether you've created your own stock portfolio or invested in a low-risk index tracker or active low-risk fund. But what is the 'right' amount of turnover? It may not surprise you that my colleagues and I have researched this too. We found that 30% turnover is enough, a number far below the levels observed in today's market. Even lower than some low-volatility indices, which are perceived to be 'passive', but still require a significant amount of trading. So you need to trade according to Aristotle's golden mean. Trade little.

In fact, the best mutual fund managers are those who have strong views, but implement these patiently. In general, funds give average returns, and after fees they tend to lag the market. That is not a very reassuring fact, and it's an inconvenient truth for fund managers. Still, some managers tend to do structurally better than others. Professor Martijn Cremers found that the most patient – and moderately active – mutual fund managers are able to outperform their peers and benchmarks by some 2% per year. And, interestingly, they also have a significant exposure to low-risk stocks with attractive valuations. Sound familiar? But patience is not only a virtue when it comes to trading. Patience is also required when it comes to sticking to your investment philosophy. You will need a persistent character to win the biggest victory of all. . .

Aristotle

384 - 322 BC

Mr Middle Way says avoid extremes.

The Biggest Victory of All

WHAT'S LEFT NOW THAT WE HAVE ANALYZED *all the possible roads that lead to Rome?* Well, quite a lot actually. Outlining the roads that lead to Rome is one thing, being able to withstand all the challenges you will face while traveling is another. It's perhaps even more important to devote some time to the journey itself rather than just the destination. Because, whether you have decided to build a conservative stock portfolio yourself or have selected a low-volatility fund, the only way to succeed is to stick with your approach in good times and bad. This is important as you will need a long-term investment horizon to be able to reap the rewards of conservative stock investing. Remember, conservative stock investing offers you a long – and sometimes lonely – road to wealth, rather than a quick 'rags to riches' solution. So what to expect on the road ahead?

Personal experience really helps us to better understand abstract concepts like beauty, faith, or risk. Søren Kierkegaard, a nineteenth-century Danish philosopher, emphasized the importance of experience when discussing truth. When it comes to stock market risk, I believe you have to experience this to understand it. Risk is quite an abstract concept. You can think about it, or do some calculations. But even if you are experienced at dealing with risk, it still also influences your deeper emotions. In the end, the combination of thoughts and emotions affects your behavior. So how can we get an idea of what this investment experience feels like and how it might influence your behavior? Let's look at some challenging experiences you might encounter along the road.[1]

History can act as a good guide when it comes to being aware of the kind of scenarios you can expect in the future. As Mark Twain allegedly once noted, history does not exactly repeat itself, but it does rhyme. So I want to share my experiences of managing a conservative equity strategy and will use three market scenarios to illustrate this. You *will* encounter these three if you invest in stocks with below-average risk. The first scenario is the most dreadful scenario for all investors: a bear market. Let's define this dark period – when investors start to wonder why they ever decided to invest in stocks in the first place – as those years when the average stock went down. The second scenario is a moderate market environment when the market rises, but not by more than 15% in the course of a year. The third and brightest scenario, with annual returns over 15%, is what I label a strong bull market. These are the moments when you feel most proud of being an investor!

Going over these three scenarios can give you some idea about what you may encounter on the road ahead. As our stock market database going back to 1929 shows, historically these three scenarios all have an equal probability of occurring. Let's take a look at Figure 14.1 to see how a conservative stock portfolio performed in these three scenarios.

---

[1] The book *The Pilgrim's Progress* by John Bunyan is a 1678 Christian allegory. It describes a traveler who faces a lot of character challenges along his road to the city of salvation. The book has influenced English and US culture profoundly. I see many parallels between it and the 'pilgrimage' of the low-risk investor.

FIGURE 14.1   Conservative stocks suffer limited losses during bear markets, but lag in bull markets

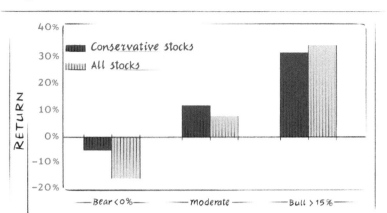

If you thought investing in conservative stocks was a water-tight strategy safeguarding you from *any* losses during bear markets, then Figure 14.1 clearly proves you wrong. In a bear market, conservative stocks also suffer some losses. The conservative stock portfolio fell by 5.4%. Although not waterproof, conservative stocks appear to be at least water resistant, as stocks across the board went down by 16.1%. Conservative stocks offer you a place to hide during bear markets as they help limit your losses.

This bear market scenario will give you mixed feelings. On the one hand, in this harsh scenario, you can be satisfied with your decision to select conservative stocks since they offer some protection. On the other hand, you did lose some money. A watertight strategy would have been to sell, as then you would have avoided the pain of any losses. So, you may have some sense of regret. Looking at how miserably your friends or colleagues have performed and being happy about it, is not very nice either. In German there is a word for this: *Schadenfreude*, which means joy about the pain of others. Moreover, in bear markets, people do not talk about the stock market much. They tend to suffer in silence, while a few might brag about how they saw this correction coming and made a brilliant move by selling all their stocks at the right moment. Bottom line: you will probably not feel the urge to start singing in the rain as a result of your relative positive performance.

Luckily for investors, bear markets don't last forever and after rain comes sunshine: the scenario of moderate market returns emerges. During these moments you will be neither happy nor unhappy with your conservative stocks, as they deliver a return which is as good as the overall return of the market. You will be rewarded for taking some stock market risk and you'll feel OK about it.

In these two scenarios, which occurred in random order, you didn't get excited and you experienced rather mixed feelings. But I can assure you that your mood will change when the bull stampedes and every investor starts to feel like a winner. At such times, when everyone else is celebrating strong market returns of over 15%, you're probably feeling like . . . a loser.

Don't get me wrong, as an investor in a conservative stock portfolio you would still have made – on average – a handsome one-year profit of over 30%. However, you would have lagged the market. Yes, you did a worse job than the average stock. What's more, at times like these, when stocks seem to only go up and risk taking is amply rewarded, you are holding on to a bag of boring low-risk stocks. Think about it: when you meet your colleagues, friends, or family and they start to talk about their huge successes on the stock market, you'll have to confess that you are that risk-shunning person who sticks to a conservative stock portfolio. Oh, and most of them won't even let you finish explaining the long-term benefits of low-risk investing, they'll just feel sorry for you. Poor you.

The main challenge is to stick to your strategy during these bullish periods. If you succeed, you're doing a great job. However, sticking with a conservative stock strategy when everybody is thrilled and enjoying the excitement of high-risk investing is a hard and lonely thing to do. The good news is that we have already limited some of this pain by including momentum in the strategy. As we have seen in the previous chapter, together with income, adding momentum increases average returns by 3% per year. Most of this return comes during this 'difficult' bullish scenario. Without the 'rule-of-three', conservative stocks would have delivered 10% less. This '10% pain relief' could be the difference between staying in and giving up.

The year 2009 proved to be a good example of such a year. It was marked by a strong market recovery that started in March and lasted throughout the rest of the year. If you had hung on to your conservative stock portfolio during that year, your return would have only been a modest 8%. While over that same period, the market returned 30%. In other words, by sticking to your conservative stock portfolio you had to forego the chance of making about 22% more in returns. In 2010, I remember a CFO and client looking back at 2009 performance and saying, "*Why did we have these conservative stocks in our pension fund last year?*"

Now, be honest for a moment and take a look at yourself in the mirror. What would you have done in such a situation? Would you have stuck to that boring, low-risk portfolio or would you have traded these stocks in and adopted another investment approach? Another investment strategy that at least performed nicely in a year like 2009? That's a tough one, isn't it? I have to confess, I remember having such feelings of regret back then.

So you will certainly encounter some pain on the road ahead. However, as they say, 'no pain, no gain'. This works in sport, but also in investing. From my own experience, I can confirm that conservative stock investing is painful, sometimes I call it the 'burnout trade'. None of the scenarios can get you really excited, and you often feel regret. So I can tell you it's a tough battle. But if these great long-term returns could be achieved without any pain, I wonder whether the paradox would exist in the first place! So, what should you do to stay invested and stay on course?

First you must understand that conservative stocks really do finish ahead, but that this only shows up over a longer investment horizon. It really is true: no long-term gain without short-term pain. You have to maintain a long-term focus, keep the faith, and be persistent. Only if you take a step back and reflect on the long-term results will you start to smile. From this perspective, increasing your investment horizon is an effective painkiller. It's OK to follow the results of your low-risk stock portfolio on a daily basis, but a less frequent assessment of your holdings may be better for your peace of mind and help you sleep at night.

But how long should this horizon be? Don't worry, you don't need nearly a century of patience to get these results. Superior long-term returns start to show up if you invest over the course of one whole investment cycle consisting of bear, moderate, and bull markets. These cycles last, on average, seven years.[2] By allowing yourself such an investment horizon, you will be able to stay focused and not get distracted by your own feelings and emotions. At the end of the cycle, you will realize that although you lagged the overall market during the steep bull markets, you may well still finish ahead because you lost less money during the bear market periods. Only by experiencing a full cycle yourself will you be able to completely understand these words: conservative stocks let you win by losing less.

Perhaps I can give you more peace of mind by looking at the risk of losing money over a multiple-year period based on our extensive dataset covering over eight decades. The risk of losing money on the stock market in any given year is about 30%, falling to 10% for a five-year horizon. This fact is often stressed by proponents of stock market investing. And now it gets even better.

---

[2] There is no exact definition of the length of a business cycle, but often the Juglar fixed-investment cycle of 7–11 years is used. According to the Hebrew narrative, Joseph correctly predicted a seven-year agricultural cycle in Egypt around 1800 BC and saved his family from starvation by also acting on this foresight.

FIGURE 14.2   Conservative stocks: the longer you hold them, the less likely you are to lose money

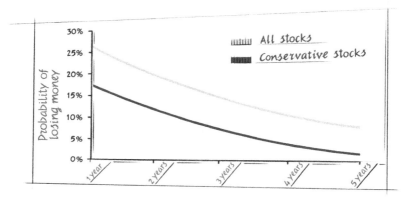

Just take a look at the graph in Figure 14.2. When you invest in conservative stocks, the risk of losing money on a one-year basis is lower: only 20%, and this falls to just 1% on a five-year basis. So you actually need less patience with conservative stocks than with average stocks.[3] That's a very comforting thought too, isn't it?

I guess that by now you understand that a conservative stock portfolio really doesn't offer you a fast, straight road to riches and that it could turn out to be a rather painful experience. During this journey your character as a conservative stock investor will be tested on numerous occasions. I would like to emphasize that it's really difficult to learn this kind of wisdom without personal experience. But if you finally reach your destination and have grown richer by investing in conservative stocks, then you should be very grateful. Grateful to yourself as you have achieved the biggest victory of all: you have conquered yourself.

---

[3] For older investors, conservative stocks are more attractive than all stocks, as they have less time to recoup any portfolio losses they have experienced.

1813–1855

"Discover truth through personal experience".

Chapter Fifteen

The Golden Rule

CAN CLASSIC WISDOM HELP US to make better investment decisions? Can virtue lead to profits? It's true, these are some thought-provoking questions. And I think the answer to these questions might be 'yes'. Moral philosophy – the study of finding out what is 'right' and what is 'wrong' behavior – could help us to have a better view, could liberate us, and it could be a guide to making the right decisions.

Before I share my perspective on how moral philosophy can be applied to investing, I need to stress something else about economics. Although it might surprise some, economics has far more to do with people than numbers. In fact, it is a *social* science. Why? Well, economists study how human beings make decisions in the interests of their own welfare. They are conscious and have had ideas about wrong and right for centuries.[1] From this perspective, the economic decisions of human beings – in their quest for welfare – depend upon their moral choices. As a matter of fact, the

---

[1] Tomas Sedlacek gives a readable account of economic history using a moral perspective in his best-selling book *Economics of Good and Evil.*

earliest economists, like Adam Smith, were moral philosophers. In other words, economics cannot exist without moral philosophy. Any economic objective, to maximize profits, sales, or wealth, has a moral foundation. Today, many people are familiar with the ideas of Adam Smith, especially the ones he expressed in *The Wealth of Nations*. In another book, *The Theory of Moral Sentiments*, he discussed the struggle we humans have between our 'passions' and our 'internal spectator'. These passions directly relate to our 'animal spirits' which are what drive markets, according to British twentieth-century economist, John Maynard Keynes. So, why am I telling you about the link between moral philosophy and economics?

Well, investigating the wisdom of classic moral philosophies can help us to tame our animal spirits and become better stock market investors. At the risk of confusing you by introducing another philosopher, I would like to bring in Confucius, a fourth-century BC Chinese philosopher.

This wise man said *"Never impose on others what you would not choose for yourself"*. This ethical rule can also be found in ancient Egyptian writings and is well known in the Western world in the somewhat more positive version of *"love your neighbor as yourself"*. It is not surprising that this saying is well known. Hillel, a first-century BC Jewish leader, summarized Judaism with this single quote. Through his teachings, but especially through his life, Jesus showed the liberating effect of radical compassion.[2] What's more, this same golden rule can be found in ancient Indian writings dating back to the eighth (!) century BC, and also plays an important role in both Hinduism and Islam. Finally, all modern philosophers, whether agnostic, atheistic, or theistic, emphasize the importance

---

[2] In 2013, the *Times* newspaper selected Jesus as the most influential person who ever lived. Quite a paradox when you give this some thought. His life was relatively short and his radical message of love made him neither famous during his lifetime nor popular with those in power. He warned that love of wealth, power, and even religion itself can lead to violations of the golden rule.

of the golden rule. In other words, all thinkers seem to agree on this one.

Now let's move on to economics. Economic models have something in common with the aforementioned moral philosophies: they are based on one fundamental assumption. It is a simple principle: people prefer more wealth to less wealth. A healthy aspiration for wealth becomes *unhealthy* when it has no limits. For example, when you want more stuff or money than you need, just for the sake of possessing it. As Aristotle already noted, too much of something good often turns into something bad. In English, an insatiable desire for wealth is called greed and is generally considered to be morally wrong. However, a moderate desire for wealth is not wrong. For example, a poor farmer who wants to earn more money to send his children to school is generally not considered immoral. So, a preference for more rather than less wealth is not morally wrong in itself. Only in an extreme form does it turn into something wrong. Therefore, from a moral point of view, this key economic assumption is not a violation of the golden rule.

However, some more recent economic models are based on another interesting assumption: people prefer to have more wealth *than others*. Is this morally wrong in itself? It might be. In some cases, comparison and envy can cause severe negative feelings, despite high absolute levels of wealth (his Ferrari has got a golden bonnet, mine only has a silver one. . .).

This underlying emotion is understandable, but in the framework of an economic model it is morally wrong. Why? Because it violates the golden ethical rule. If you become happier simply because someone else is doing badly or worse than you are, then you are on shaky moral ground. The reverse is also true – if your neighbor's good fortune is making you unhappy, then you are violating the golden rule too. All moral philosophies warn against this vice. Even in moderation, jealousy and envy are bad. 'Mr Middle Way' Aristotle also denounced envy.

Back to financial economics. One of the most famous financial economic models is the Capital Asset Pricing Model (CAPM), which won a Nobel Prize in 1990. This is the model that predicts a positive and linear relationship between risk and return. I will spare you all the details, but this model makes a couple of assumptions about people and their behavior. For example, it assumes people prefer more to less and *do not compare* their wealth with others. So the CAPM has some decent moral assumptions: people prefer more wealth to less and do not compare. It also assumes an absolute view on wealth, where happiness is not distorted by the wealth of other investors. So the behavioral assumption underpinning this famous model does not violate the golden ethical rule.

However, as you have now already witnessed in the first chapters of this book, the theoretical CAPM fails miserably to describe the actual relationship between risk and return. It describes a perfect world that doesn't seem to exist. As a result, many researchers have declared the model dead, including one of its early proponents. So, if the CAPM is a washed-up empirical failure, why do we still use it? Interestingly, at most finance faculties around the world the model is still taught as part of the standard curriculum. Even when I teach at university, I use this model.[3] One could, therefore, state that the model is still alive. But why? Why would anyone – including me – use a model which has been declared dead?

Let me explain this. Yes, the model fails to describe reality as it really *is*; the CAPM does not describe how the world works. But it can be used as a tool for how things *should* be. There is an important and sometimes subtle difference between 'is' and 'should'. Although the model does not describe how most people *do* behave, it can be used to describe how they *should* behave. If most investors do violate the golden rule and compare themselves with others all

---

[3] The CAPM can also be used to better understand the investment paradox. See, for example, Blitz, Falkenstein, and van Vliet (2014).

the time, that does not make this behavior good. This unhealthy comparison is an explanation for the risk–return paradox. We have seen that a *relative* risk framework dominates the financial industry and that most investors *do compare* themselves too much with others. This collective 'vice' can cause a good model based on sound principles to fail to work. But that doesn't mean it still can't prove to be very useful.

I believe you should use the CAPM because this model tells you which investment decision is right and which investment decision is wrong. It is a good tool to help you make wise and rational decisions. For example, the model is useful for firms comparing different internal investment projects. When two projects have the same expected profit and all other things are equal, a low-risk project should take preference over one that involves higher risk. Also, when selecting the right investment fund, the CAPM can be a good guide. If a mutual fund has shown a high return over a certain period, it is wise to ask yourself whether this was achieved with a higher or lower level of risk exposure. Finally, the CAPM can also help fund managers select stocks. If two stocks pay the same dividend and have the same business momentum and growth, they should buy the low-risk stock rather than the high-risk one. Although, according to the CAPM theory, these stocks should not exist, in reality they do. As we have seen throughout this book, conservative stocks make you wealthy, whereas risky stocks make you poor.

Let's use an analogy here with health. In theory, to be healthy everyone should exercise for at least 30 minutes a day; this is a good health model. However, in practice most people are too passive and do not exercise enough. Although the model does not describe how people actually behave, does this mean the theory is wrong and you should stop exercising? The answer is no. It is a good guideline for how people should behave. The same goes with this finance model. The CAPM is dead, long live the CAPM!

In other words, this book is about people who do not always behave according to theory. We simply have to accept that the stock market is driven by people and their emotions and their desire to compare. Interestingly, this fact of life creates opportunities for those who can control their 'passions' and 'animal spirits' and show virtue. In the case of investing, investors could simply start by following the ancient golden rule and stop comparing. By doing this, classical wisdom would help you to make better investment decisions. You would then be in a position to achieve high returns from low-risk stocks. Quite a paradox, isn't it?

Confucius

551 - 479 BC

"*Never impose on others what you would not choose for yourself*".

Chapter Sixteen

The Paradox Is Everywhere

LOW-RISK STOCKS BEAT HIGH-RISK STOCKS: an inconvenient truth. Inconvenient, as these results prove that the standard models are wrong. Despite these results, it is still commonly accepted wisdom – and assumed in basically all finance models and textbooks – that more risk *should* lead to higher returns. But it does not. Time to say goodbye to this common investment wisdom?

Maybe. But let's pause for a minute – and please remain skeptical – to take a broader perspective and look at some more evidence. Because maybe backward-looking statistical measures such as volatility or beta are not the best ways to capture or measure stock risk. Is the investment paradox robust when other, more fundamental risk measures are used? Let's have a look at financial leverage. A highly financial leveraged company relies more on debt than equity to finance its operations and therefore exposes the equity investor to more risk. The evidence? Stocks with higher financial leverage also have below-average returns.[1] In general,

---

[1] Penman, Richardson, and Tuna (2007).

stocks that have a higher probability of running into a financially distressful situation (like a default), measured in various dimensions, also have lower returns.[2] These findings add to the robustness of our results as the 'inconvenient truth' does not critically depend on the exact definition of risk.

Looking at the robust, long-term evidence for US stocks, you could conclude that higher risk doesn't result in higher returns when investing in US stocks. As most academic research studies focus on US data, while the majority of the global equity market is outside the US, it begs the question whether the paradox also prevails on international stock markets. Well, it does. Robert Haugen shows that low-risk stocks beat high-risk stocks in *33 countries* around the world.[3] David Blitz and I also show evidence for this in European, Japanese, and emerging stock markets. What's more, deep historical evidence shows that low-risk stocks outperformed high-risk stocks on the Belgian stock market going back as far as 1873![4]

Another way to study the risk–return relationship is to consider groups of stocks. For example, stocks grouped in countries, sectors, or even mutual funds. Elroy Dimson used 107 years of data for 17 international stock markets. His research gave various fascinating results including the fact that risky stock markets do not give higher returns than low-risk markets.[5] What about stocks grouped in industries? Together with Ronald Doeswijk, I constructed a global database and found that cyclical sectors do not outperform defensive sectors.[6] Joop Huij studied the risk and return of mutual funds. He wondered if mutual funds, which invested in low-risk stocks, performed better than funds which did

---

[2] Campbell, Hilscher, and Szilagyi (2008).
[3] Baker and Haugen (2012).
[4] Annaert and Mensah (2014).
[5] Dimson, Marsh, and Staunton (2011).
[6] Doeswijk and van Vliet (2011).

not invest in low-risk stocks. You will probably not be surprised by the answer to this question. They do perform better.[7]

One funny human trait is that once you are aware of something, you suddenly start seeing it everywhere. First you didn't notice it, but once you have discovered it, you find confirmation everywhere. For example, if someone close to you is pregnant, you suddenly see pregnant women everywhere. Or when you discover a new cool car, you suddenly tend to keep seeing it driving around all over the place. The same goes for the investment paradox. Once you are aware of it, you will become amazed by the enormous amount of evidence that there is for it all around you. And then you wonder why you were not aware of this paradox before.

Let's consider some more evidence. What about other asset classes? For example, what about investing in bonds, currencies, or commodities? These are all major and multi-trillion-dollar markets, just like the stock market. Let's start with bonds. Bonds are generally less risky investments than stocks. Just think about it: as a bond investor you lend your money to a company (or country) which gives you a periodic coupon payment in return, and your investment back when the debt matures. Usually, the longer the lending period or maturity, the higher the coupon. A longer maturity also means higher risk, as your bond is more sensitive to rising interest rates. As a result, bond investors generally demand a higher coupon for taking on more risk.

Besides maturity, creditworthiness is another dimension of risk for bond and equity investors. The biggest risk for bond investors is that the company defaults and they don't get their money back. In order to help investors cope with this risk, credit rating agencies like Moody's and Standard and Poor's (S&P) classify the riskiness of companies by assigning them credit scores. So-called 'junk' bonds or high-yield bonds have a higher risk than so-called 'investment

---

[7] Gelderen and Huij (2014).

grade' bonds. Do these riskier bonds have higher returns than low-risk bonds? The short answer is no. Although junk bonds do give a higher coupon, this extra income doesn't make up for the higher number of defaults.[8] So, while climbing the risk ladder as a bond investor, taking more risk is not rewarded with more return. My colleague Patrick Houweling has been studying the corporate bond market for about two decades now. He manages a multi-billion family of funds which invest in low-risk corporate bonds. In his research he has found that low-risk bonds have high risk-adjusted returns and that income and momentum are powerful factors as well, as was the case in our results for the equity market.[9] So, even when investing in corporate bonds, do not ignore the law of three.

And what about commodities? In this massive market, most of the trading is carried out using derivatives on the future prices of commodities such as oil, copper, gold, wheat, or even pork bellies. A precious metal like gold is a more conservative commodity than an energy like gas, which is more volatile. Do high-risk commodities also generate better returns than low-risk ones? I hope I'm not starting to boring you, but the answer – once again – is a convincing 'no.'[10]

Let's move over to other derivatives and focus on options. Mankind has been trading options for centuries, in fact they can be traced to ancient times with references to options dating back to early Greek and Chinese writings. Nowadays these instruments are sometimes referred to as the 'poor man's stock'; when you have a strong view but lack the money to invest in the underlying security, you can get yourself an option instead. Interestingly, options give low returns and the riskier the options, the lower the returns. Again, in the options market there is evidence for a negative relationship between risk and return.[11]

---

[8] Altman and Bana (2004).
[9] Houweling and van Zundert (2015).
[10] Blitz and De Groot (2014).
[11] Ni (2008).

Lottery tickets resemble options in several ways. Small investments can yield very high returns. Just think of the strip in Las Vegas or the Macau skyline and you'll understand that a lot of money is spent on gambling. Besides fun, these gambling 'markets' give us a further opportunity to learn about human behavior and which type of risks we like the most. Both in lotteries and horse racing there is a so-called 'long-shot' bias. This refers to the tendency of gamblers to overvalue those bets which have a very small probability of occurring, but if they do occur, the payout is very high. In other words, low probability but potential high payout. These bets seem to be irresistible to most people. Snowberg and Wolfers looked at a dataset of over 200,000 horse races and found an average return of -23% for all horse race bets, which falls to -61% for the most risky long-shots.[12] Again, on the horse track, 'high risk doesn't equal high return'.

The paradox is also visible in other markets. For example, in the Hollywood movie business, risk is not rewarded.[13] In private equity, more conservative 'buy-out funds' outperform riskier venture capital investments.[14] Houses are risky investments, but they often fail to keep pace with inflation after maintenance costs have been taken into account. For those interested in this topic, Eric Falkenstein's book, *The Missing Risk Premium: Why Low Volatility Investing Works*, discusses these and several other examples in more detail.

The evidence is everywhere and it is not confined to one small section of one particular market.[15] Stock markets around

---

[12] Snowberg and Wolfers (2010). The authors also test if gamblers really like the outcome of winning a lot of money, or if they have a misperception of the chance of winning this amount. They show that misperception of risk better explains behavior, which falsifies the Expected Utility Theory and is in line with the Cumulative Prospect Theory.
[13] De Vany (2004).
[14] Phalippou and Gottschalg (2009).
[15] Frazzini and Pedersen (2014).

the world, mutual funds, bond markets, commodity markets, and option markets: the investment paradox pops up everywhere. In all these markets, taking on more risk does not lead to higher returns. However, one should not fall victim to the confirmation bias.[16] Yes, risk is not rewarded within all these individual markets. But *across* some markets, like the bond and stock markets, taking a little market risk can lead to higher returns. First, by investing in more conservative bonds with short maturities and good credit ratings. In the long term, these low-risk bonds outperform a lower risk alternative such as a savings account. Second, by investing in low-risk stocks. Conservative stocks also outperform lower risk asset classes like bonds or cash. So *within* virtually all markets, risk is not rewarded. However, *across* the two asset classes of bonds and equities there is a modest reward for risk.[17]

I hope that all this evidence does not cause you to become an extremely risk-averse investor. That is not my intention. Remember the golden mean: true virtue can often be found between the two extremes. Risk is not bad in all cases, but please be aware that it is not rewarded in *almost* all cases. As a rule of thumb, avoid anything that looks like a lottery ticket or promises you a very high return. Do not place long-shot bets, not at the horse track and not in your investment portfolio. And let's remember the good news. You can make a positive return and increase your wealth by taking on *some* limited risk within the bond and equity markets.

---

[16] The confirmation bias is the tendency to search for, interpret, favor, and recall information in a way that confirms one's preexisting beliefs or hypotheses. See also Wikipedia: https://en.wikipedia.org/wiki/Confirmation_bias.

[17] This existence of a positive bond premium and equity premium suggests that investors are risk averse in the asset allocation decision phase (phase I), but change behavior when they select securities within these markets (phase II). Although many investors behave like this, this is not assumed in models like the Capital Asset Pricing Model.

Will the Paradox Persist?

Søren Kierkegaard once stated: *"Life can only be understood backwards, but should be lived forwards"*. Throughout this book we have spent most of the time looking backwards in order to better understand the paradox and to see whether we could use it to build an investment strategy. But let's leave history aside for a moment and focus on the future instead. What does the future hold for a paradox investor? What will happen if everybody starts buying conservative stocks and shunning high-risk stocks? Could the investment paradox disappear?

Yes. This is possible, but not very likely. In fact, the paradox could even become stronger over time. Although the future of conservative stock investing is uncertain, we can try to make some projections. Let's start by highlighting again why the investment paradox exists. It exists because it is caused by the behavior of market participants. First you have to *see* it, second you should be *able* to apply it, and third you have to be *willing* to profit from it. Let's look at these three requirements.

See It

An increasing number of studies on the paradox and the growth in the number of low-volatility funds clearly indicate that the paradox is being noticed by more and more investors. This book reveals the existence of the paradox, and if a lot of investors buy and read it, awareness of the paradox will increase still more. As a consequence, the group of investors who are still *unaware* of this paradox is gradually shrinking. This development could result in the gradual disappearance of the paradox in the future if all investors who 'see' the paradox also act on it. This is quite straightforward; now let's look at the second requirement.

Be Able to Exploit It

Of those who see it, not many can profit from it. It is important to know that until the 1990s, most stocks were directly owned and managed by investors. However, in recent decades there has been more of a division between the people who *own* stocks and the people who *manage* them. Currently, a large and increasing part of the stock market is owned by collective investment schemes like pension funds or sovereign wealth funds. At the same time, more money is being allocated to mutual funds and ETFs. As a result, professional investment managers now account for a large and increasing part of the total stock market. Asset management firms are primarily concerned with revenues and profits. But the portfolio managers who work for them are more concerned about something else. Remember from Chapter 6 that they tend to be concerned about their own careers and are paid to *take* risk, rather than to *reduce* it. This means that only an increasingly small part of the market is able to profit from the paradox. This is fully understandable and will continue as long as fund managers have to consistently outperform their benchmarks. From their perspective, conservative stocks will continue to be 'risky' and will therefore be shunned, irrespective of whether they are fully aware of the existence of the investment paradox or not.

Perhaps you are wondering if anything can change this situation? Well, something simple could change the current status quo. For example, if *performance* benchmarks were replaced by *risk* benchmarks, things could possibly start to change. But is this likely to happen any time soon? At this moment there are no signs that this is happening or will happen in the near future, mainly because it is quite challenging to define risk. The short memory of investors doesn't help. Although directly after a crisis, like the one we saw in 2008, most investors seem to be more aware of risk, this fear quickly subsides once markets recover and start to rally again. The anguish of a bear market is soon forgotten and any focus on risk quickly switches back to a focus on returns and outperformance. Let's not forget the regulators, as their influence on stock prices is increasing as well. According to their frameworks, all stocks have an equal amount of risk, which is a simple but dangerous premise. This creates an incentive for professional investors to take on more risk, without being penalized for buying risky stocks.

These trends of increased regulation and the prevalence of professional investors managing money will contribute to the sustainability of the paradox. Another, more obvious trend that will sustain the paradox is the growth of investment in passive market-weighted indices. Investors who decide to track market indices also actively choose not to be able to profit from it. If these trends continue, we can expect the paradox to become even stronger in the future.

Be Willing to Do It

You might see it and you might be able to take advantage of it, but you have to be willing to do so. Many investors are driven towards the riskiest part of the stock market by a mix of hope and overconfidence. They tend to overpay for 'lottery-type' stocks as they believe they could either make them rich or create a great story. Just remember my Fokker adventure: this risk-seeking behavior often ends in tears. However, there is not so much we can do about this. Our risk-seeking behavior is fully understandable and driven by deep human instincts.

What's more, you also need to be quite patient and willing and able to invest for a full market cycle. As I have explained earlier in Chapter 13, patience is a virtue which many people lack: *we want it all and we want it now!* We tend to be way too active on the stock market and trade too much. If we put all this human behavior together, I believe our traits and instincts are not likely to change and this will sustain the existence of the investment paradox. Hegel – this time I'm quoting a German philosopher – already noted that *what history teaches us is that we tend not to learn from history.*

First see it, then be able to take advantage of it, and finally be willing to invest in the paradox. In a nutshell, these are the three conditions that have to be met before anyone starts to invest in these kinds of stocks. Perhaps this explains why the assets invested in these strategies are still limited while the paradox was first discovered over 40 years ago. I think that even though it may well become more well known, there is every reason to believe the paradox will continue to exist and may even become stronger.

Chapter Eighteen

Final Reflections

BLAISE PASCAL, a seventeenth-century philosopher, once remarked: "*I would have written a shorter letter, but I did not have the time*". Another paradox which I like a lot and which has made me try to keep this story as short as possible and its contents 'as simple as possible, but not simpler'. I will conclude with some final thoughts and personal reflections.

Besides evidence-based investing, another thing that fascinates me is historically, especially long-term economic history covering centuries of civilization. From this perspective, the stock market evidence presented in this book is relatively short, as it only goes back to the 1920s. Although it's quite an extensive period, it contains a limited number of full business cycles. Interestingly, the oldest institutions in the world aren't companies. Firms – which often aim to increase profits – have average lifespans of only decades. In fact, only a few listed companies have been around for more than a hundred years.[1] In contrast, academic institutions – which aim to increase knowledge – have lifespans that easily stretch over several centuries. The oldest university in Bologna is over 900 years old and Plato's academy lasted for many centuries. In addition, some institutes have even longer lifespans. For example, several oriental churches have existed for nearly two millennia and the wisdom of Aristotle and Confucius still inspires many people even after 2,500 years.

Profit-seeking companies and *wisdom-seeking* philosophies have a different impact horizon, and wisdom clearly beats profit. According to the Bible, King Solomon first chooses wisdom above all other things. Because he makes the right decision, he ends up with wealth and power too. I believe the order here is right. Wisdom is needed to rightly manage wealth and power.

So where does this place me as a fund manager, managing other people's money? How do I balance wisdom and wealth? Well, first of all, my job exists only because our clients put their faith in us. You need faith to make a decision and wisdom to make the right decision. I want to ensure that our clients feel they have made a wise decision by choosing us to manage their money. Several principles help to safeguard their funds.

First, fund management is a team effort. This helps to make all the decisions transparent and subject to criticism. Second, we rely on a common investment philosophy. We use an evidence-based approach to investigate what works on the stock market and translate this knowledge into a prudent and understandable investment strategy. Third, we put our money where our mouth is and practice

---

[1] Stock markets are a relatively modern-day phenomenon, with the first public listing taking place in 1602. The Dutch East India Company was the first company in the world to issue public shares on the Amsterdam Bourse. In pre-modern times, shares of public companies, known as *publicani*, were traded at the Forum in Rome. Among non-listed firms, some Japanese firms have existed for more than a millennium. Kongo Gumi was founded in 578 and ceased to exist in 2006. Interestingly, this firm constructed Buddhist temples, serving wisdom seekers.

what we preach by investing in the funds we manage. For example, the large majority of my personal assets are invested in the Conservative Equity funds, diversified across hundreds of stocks. Finally, the funds are evaluated over periods of multiple years and on a risk-adjusted basis. This latter phenomenon is quite exceptional in the asset management industry. These shared principles create a balance and enable me to sleep at night.

In addition to this, there is something else that gives me a sense of purpose. It is the knowledge that the market might become a bit more efficient by investing in those low-risk stocks that do not receive enough capital from other investors. I believe this is important, as a stock market that functions properly has proven to be important for the health and wealth of nations.

I find my deepest sense of purpose on a personal level. In my daily existence I find happiness in trying to pursue a virtuous life. I believe that love is the most important virtue, more important even than the virtues mentioned earlier on. In the fast world of finance it is important to stay serene and take a step back at regular intervals. For me, simply sticking to the golden rule creates interdependence and is an assignment big enough to keep me happily occupied for the rest of my life.

And where does all this leave you, dear reader? Well, you have discovered that low-risk stocks beat high-risk stocks. You have seen quite some evidence for this investment paradox. Once you are aware of it, you suddenly see it everywhere, all around you. Invest patiently and avoid anything 'fast' like a hare. The best way to succeed is to stick to the rule of three. Consider risk, income, and momentum when selecting stocks or other securities.

But the rule of three can also be applied to the way you invest as a person. *First,* experience conservative stock investing yourself for a couple of years and let Kierkegaard inspire you to claim the biggest victory of all. *Second,* apply the golden ethical rule and stop comparing your performance with that of others. Embrace some

Confucian wisdom, as this will probably make you happier and wealthier. *Third*, remember the golden mean. Let Aristotle help you to take an optimal amount of risk – not too much and also not too little. Extreme risk-averse behavior is not good either; there have to be some investors who are still prepared to buy risky stocks. But, I would recommend anyone to steer well away from failing Dutch aircraft manufacturers...

Let me finish by expressing my hope that some of the insights shared in this book will help you become a wiser investor. My father read the story and felt honored to be its first reader. He also understood the message and liked the metaphors and personal anecdotes. Our kids get a smile on their faces and start dancing when I say the word 'volatility' at home. Finally, my sweet wife teasingly remarked that I look more handsome in the picture below than I look in real life...

Hopefully this story on risk and return has made you wonder but has also made you smile.

Pim van Vliet

Jan's Perspective

*W*AIT A SECOND. *Haven't I just finished reading a book on risk and return written by a Dutch fund manager named Pim? So who's Jan and why should I bother about his perspective?*

Yes, you've just read Pim's views on risk and return and their implications for investing and life in general. But, to be honest, you weren't alone when he told you this story of the paradox of 'low risk gives high returns'. Quite the contrary in fact, as, throughout the book, I was there *too*. With you and *for* you. You see, although Pim is easy going, he can sometimes get a bit too serious and philosophical. So I urged him to deliver what is a serious message in a relaxed, sometimes funny and upbeat tone in order to keep you with us right to the end of the book. So who am I?

Well, I started investing when I was a young teenager, putting my savings in fancy and risky stocks. I basically started out as a kind of momentum investor in the late 1990s having discovered that some stocks could easily double in price in short periods of time. As a result, I found myself scanning the newspaper for stocks trading at new 52-week highs and with '.com' in their names. In my quest to become a rich investor, I also discovered the 'art' of technical analysis. As the value of my holdings grew rapidly, I started to believe that studying price charts was my road to riches. I read dozens of books on this topic, got myself a qualification in this field, and even had a thriving business as a writer and online publisher of stock market newsletters. Despite this success, by the time I graduated from university I realized that – given the actual value of my brokerage account – I was actually better at selling newsletters than applying a momentum strategy. My hare-hunting activities on the stock market also badly affected my well-being as an investor. I was impatient, traded a lot, and was always afraid I might miss out on a price quotation or newsflash. It was time to find a different investment style.

I continued to follow my quest by reading the biographies of successful investors. I quickly discovered that most of them had a different investment philosophy: they focused on income when selecting value stocks. Armed with this information, I – once again – plundered the shelves of online book stores, became a certified analyst, and, a few years later, a fund manager; I found myself studying balance sheets while keeping one eye on price trends. Adopting the principles of value investing and sticking to them had a positive effect on my investment behavior, as I had to learn to be patient if my investments were to work out.

Did I care about risk in those days? For sure! Just like every-one else I hated to lose the money I had invested. But I also still believed that risk was a necessary ingredient for investment success. I had learned this at university and observed that, across various markets, risk was rewarded. Some years later, while managing the investments of pension funds and insur-ance companies, I came across the concept of low-risk investing. I realized how clients could benefit from this risk-based invest-ment approach. Despite the appealing investment results of this approach, I had never personally experienced the effect investing in a low-risk strategy would have on my behavior as an investor.

Given my experience with momentum and income investing, I was also a bit skeptical to declare this investment style to be my new 'holy grail'.

All the pieces came together when I joined Robeco a few years ago. The company had already been successfully applying academic findings on momentum, value, and low risk to its investment strategies for years. When I joined the team I experienced my own 'Eureka' moment, as I saw not only the academic proof, but also the living proof of how effective these insights are when *combined* together into prudent investment strategies. I realized that my doubts as to whether a single investment method (e.g. momentum or income) could offer the best solution were completely justified.

Because there isn't one single best investment method. Yes, it is best to avoid high-risk stocks if possible. And income and momentum strategies also give good results. However, instead of focusing on one, you probably will be happier (and wealthier!) if you just maintain a broader perspective and avoid extremes. Try to seek out the best in each strategy and combine them together in one approach. This is why I am such a big fan of the conservative stock formula we described in Chapter 9. It takes the best concepts from low-risk investing and combines them with income and momentum to create one elegant and successful formula.

However, it's not the elements of the conservative stock formula or the financial results it produces that bring me the most joy. There is something that is more important to me. Once you start applying the formula, you not only become more aware of the paradoxes in your daily life, it also allows you to become a more relaxed investor. Once you realize that you only need a moderate amount of risk in your portfolio and you maintain a long-term perspective, you will automatically be less inclined to check stock quotes, wait for newsflashes, trade a lot, and so on. The formula has transformed a former hare hunter into a more mature investor who appreciates steady tortoises!

Shortly after my own 'Eureka' moment, I began to realize that this investment paradox could help many investors worldwide, if they knew of its existence. I wanted to help investors like you and me to become aware of the investment paradox, so they could apply it to their own portfolios as well. To help them invest more wisely, to be more 'tortoise-like'. Luckily for me, Pim shared the same vision. As he was experienced in writing for an academic audience and I had written a lot of material for investors like us, we decided to join forces.

Writing this book has proved to be an enjoyable and satisfying journey, full of the wisdom and ideas that Pim has shared with me along the way. It has also been a very personal experience, as we have had to disclose to each other our worst investment mistakes and innermost feelings. Given our different backgrounds, we have also corrected each other a lot. Pim thought I added too many jokes and exclamation marks, while I had to press the 'delete' key now and then to make sure we didn't lose you completely somewhere in the middle of the book! I believe – in the spirit of Aristotle – we've found each other in the middle. Together we had no shortage of material, probably enough for three books (!), so a certain amount of compromise was required.

And yes, I also hope this book has not only got you smiling and made you wonder, but that it also proves to be beneficial to the value of your investment portfolio. However, after reading dozens of investment books, I can honestly say that ancient wisdom, philosophical ideas, and virtues are more likely to help you be a successful investor than any new investment book (including this one) is. That's another paradox!

Jan de Koning

Appendix

ParadoxInvesting.com

Now you that you know all about it, we hope you will be able and willing to practically implement this prudent investment philosophy. We're grateful you have taken the time to 'listen' to the story of this remarkable investment paradox. And although we are nearing the end of this book, the story of low-risk investing is far from over.

Think about it: despite the fact that evidence for low-risk investing dates back to 1873, investors have only just begun to apply this philosophy to their equity portfolios. Low-risk investing is still in its infancy when compared to a proven and widely known investment style like value investing, and many investors still need to open their eyes. We expect an increasing number of people to become aware of the paradox and for new research insights and investment products to follow accordingly. Neither do we rule out the possibility that we will have some new ideas and opinions to share with you at some point in the future.

The story of paradox investing continues online at www.paradoxinvesting.com. This website lists an overview of different stock and ETF screening websites. The dataset (in Excel) that we've used throughout this book is also available on this website, so you can download it and try to falsify the existence of the investment paradox yourself. Please give it a try!

Acknowledgments

I REMEMBER THE DAY THAT JAN APPROACHED ME and said we should write a book on low-risk investing. We were both familiar with many popular books on investing and none had yet introduced this particular investment style to a broader audience. We decided to go ahead and, during this process, which lasted about a year, we traveled this road together. Thanks for your companionship, Jan!

A small army – about 40 people – has contributed to this book by supporting us, editing the manuscript, or giving useful feedback. First, we would like to thank Niek van Vliet, Kees de Koning, Aaldert Gooijer, Jaap-Jan van Ingen, Cateline Lima, and Tim Oskam. Your feedback has helped us to ensure that this book is more accessible to a broader audience. Second, thanks to research colleagues Milan Vidojevic, Patrick Houweling, Matthias Hanauer, Weili Zhou, Wilma de Groot, and Joop Huij who contributed to the academic input that underpins our arguments and helped us provide empirical evidence. A special thank you to David Blitz, my co-author on many academic articles on this topic. Your feedback encouraged us to make the story appealing to experts like you as well. Third, special thanks to our marketing colleague Laurens Masereeuw for helping us present the story in the most attractive way. In addition, colleagues Peter van Kleef, Margret Smits, John van der Moezel and Robin van der Poel, who kept us on the right track. Fourth, portfolio managers Jan-Sytze Mosse-laar, Maarten Polfliet, Rob van Bommel, Arnoud Klep, and client portfolio managers Tom Naaijkens, Frank Wirds, and Bernhard Breloer. You have all helped us to structure this book given your own experience of explaining the conservative equity investment philosophy to our clients. Thank you all for your time and your useful suggestions.

Thanks also to Peter Ferket, Hans Rademaker, Hester Borrie, Edwin Rietkerk and Arlette van Ditshuizen for your general support on this project. Gerben de Zwart, Laurens Swinkels, Jasper Haak, and Artino Janssen, thanks for your early belief in the paradox and your support to launch a Conservative Equity fund back in 2005. Eric Falkenstein and Han Smit, thanks for sharing your experiences with writing and publishing a book. Petra Sagel, Marc van der Holst, and Sarah Hammond thanks for your help during the editing process. Gemma Valler and Stephen Mullaly, thanks for your support and input from Wiley publishers, including finding a good book title. Finally, Ron Offerman, thank you for the beautiful illustrations which support our story in a very appealing way. We just hope our craftsmanship matches yours.

References

Altman, E. & Bana, G. (2004), Defaults and Returns on High-Yield Bonds, *Journal of Portfolio Management*, 30(2), 59–73.

Ang, A., Hodrick, R.J., Xing, Y., & Zhang, X. (2006), The Cross-Section of Volatility and Expected Returns, *Journal of Finance*, 61, 259–299.

Annaert, J. & Mensah, L. (2014), Cross-sectional Predictability of Stock Returns: Evidence from the 19th Century Brussels Stock Exchange (1873–1914), *Explorations in Economic History*, 52, 22–43.

Aristotle, *Nicomachean Ethics*, translated by J.A.K. Thomson, Penguin Classics 2003.

Baker, N. & Haugen, R.A. (2012), Low Risk Stocks Outperform within All Observable Markets of the World, SSRN Working Paper, 2055431.

Barber, B.M. & Odean, T. (2001), Boys Will Be Boys: Gender, Overconfidence, and Common Stock Investment, *Quarterly Journal of Economics*, 116, 261–292.

Basu, S. (1977), Investment Performance of Common Stocks in Relation to their Price–Earnings Ratios: A Test of the Efficient Market Hypothesis, *Journal of Finance*, 32(3), 663–682.

Bernstein, P. (1998), *Against the Gods: The Remarkable Story of Risk*, John Wiley & Sons, Ltd.

Blitz, D., Falkenstein, E., & van Vliet, P. (2014), Explanations for the Volatility Effect: An Overview Based on the CAPM Assumptions, *Journal of Portfolio Management*, Spring, 61–76.

Blitz, D. & De Groot, W. (2014), Strategic Allocation to Commodity Factor Premiums, *Journal of Alternative Investments*, 12, 51–60.

Blitz, D., Pang, J., & van Vliet, P. (2011), The Volatility Effect in Emerging Markets, *Emerging Markets Review*, 16, 31–45.

Blitz, D. & van Vliet, P. (2007), The Volatility Effect: Lower Risk Without Lower Return, *Journal of Portfolio Management*, Fall, 102–113.

Bunyan, J. (1678), *The Pilgrim's Progress from This World to That Which is to Come*, Dover 2003.

Campbell, J., Hilscher, J., & Szilagyi, J. (2008), In Search of Distress Risk, *Journal of Finance*, 63(6), 2899–2939.

Cremers, M. & Pareek, A. (2016), Patient Capital Outperformance: The Investment Skill of High Active Share Managers Who Trade Infrequently, forthcoming, *Journal of Financial Economics*.

De Vany, A. (2004), *Hollywood Economics: How Extreme Uncertainty Shapes the Film Industry*, Routledge.

Dimson, E., Marsh, P., & Staunton, M. (2002), *Triumph of the Optimists: 101 Years of Global Investment Returns*, Princeton University Press.

Dimson, E., Marsh, P., & Staunton, M. (2011), Equity Premiums around the World, *Research Foundation Publications*, 2011(4).

Doeswijk, R. & van Vliet, P. (2011), Global Tactical Asset Allocation: A Quantitative Approach, *Journal of Portfolio Management*, 38(1), 29–47.

Falkenstein, E. (2009), *Finding Alpha: The Search for Alpha When Risk and Return Break Down*, John Wiley & Sons, Ltd.

Falkenstein, E. (2012), *The Missing Risk Premium: Why Low Volatility Investing Works*, CreateSpace Independent Publishing Platform.

Fama, E.F. & French, K.R. (1996), The CAPM is Wanted, Dead or Alive, *Journal of Finance*, 51(5), 1947–1958.

Frazzini, A. & Pedersen, L. (2014), Betting against Beta, *Journal of Financial Economics*, 111(1), 1–25.

French, K. (2008), The Cost of Active Investing, *Journal of Finance*, 63, 1537–1573.

Gelderen, E. & Huij, J. (2014), Academic Knowledge Dissemination in the Mutual Fund Industry: Can Mutual Funds Successfully Adopt Factor Investing Strategies? *Journal of Portfolio Management*, 40(4), 157–167.

Goetzmann, W. & Huang, S. (2015), Momentum in Imperial Russia, SSRN Working Paper, 2663482.

Haugen, R. (2001), *The Inefficient Stock Market: What Pays Off and Why*, Pearson.

Houweling, P. & van Zundert, J. (2015), Factor Investing in the Corporate Bond Market, SSRN Working Paper, 2516322.

Jegadeesh, N. & Titman, S. (1993), Returns to Buying Winners and Selling Losers: Implications for Stock Market Efficiency, *Journal of Finance*, 48(1), 65–91.

Kahneman, D. (2011), *Thinking, Fast and Slow*, Farrar, Straus and Giroux.

Karceski, J. (2002), Returns-Chasing Behavior, Mutual Funds, and Beta's Death, *Journal of Financial and Quantitative Analysis*, 37(4).

Kumar, A. (2009), Who Gambles in the Stock Market? *Journal of Finance*, 64(4), 1889–1933.

Lynch, P. (2000), *One Up On Wall Street: How to Use What You Already Know to Make Money in the Market*, Simon & Schuster.

Markowitz, H. (1952), Portfolio Selection, *Journal of Finance*, 7(1), 77–91.

Montier, J. (2010), *The Little Book of Behavioral Investing: How Not to be Your Own Worst Enemy*, John Wiley & Sons, Ltd.

Ni, S. (2008), Stock Options Returns: A Puzzle, SSRN Working Paper, 959024.

Penman, S., Richardson, S., & Tuna, I. (2007), The Book-to-Price Effect in Stock Returns: Accounting for Leverage, *Journal of Accounting Research*, 45(2), 427–467.

Phalippou, L. & Gottschalg, O. (2009), The Performance of Private Equity Funds, *Review of Financial Studies*, 22(4), 1747–1776.

Sedlacek, T. (2013), *Economics of Good and Evil: The Quest for Economic Meaning from Gilgamesh to Wall Street*, Oxford University Press.

Smith, A. (1759), *The Theory of Moral Sentiments*, reprinted by Penguin 2010.

Snowberg, E. & Wolfers, J. (2010), Explaining the Favorite Longshot Bias: Is it Risk-Love or Misperceptions? National Bureau of Economic Research Working Paper, 15923.

Svenson, O. (1981), Are We All Less Risky and More Skillful Than Our Fellow Drivers? *Acta Psychologica*, 47(2), 143–148.

Taleb, N. (2007), *The Black Swan: The Impact of the Highly Improbable*, Random House.

van Vliet, P. (2004), Downside Risk and Empirical Asset Pricing, PhD thesis, Erasmus University Rotterdam.

Index

Compiled by Marian Preston at Preston Indexing, 26 Park Lane, Southwick, Brighton BN42 4DL.